The Ego's Echo

The Universal Life Cycle—
The Journey of an Embracing Leader

awaken the universe within

Who am I?

Willem de Liefde

BALBOA
PRESS

A DIVISION OF HAY HOUSE

Balboa Press books may be ordered through booksellers or by contacting:

Balboa Press
A Division of Hay House
1663 Liberty Drive
Bloomington, IN 47403
www.balboapress.com
1 (877) 407-4847

Because of the dynamic nature of the Internet, any web addresses or links contained in
this book may have changed since publication and may no longer be valid. The views
expressed in this work are solely those of the author and do not necessarily reflect the views
of the publisher, and the publisher hereby disclaims any responsibility for them.

The author of this book does not dispense medical advice or prescribe the use of any technique as a form of
treatment for physical, emotional, or medical problems without the advice of a physician, either directly or
indirectly. The intent of the author is only to offer information of a general nature to help you in your quest
for emotional and spiritual well-being. In the event you use any of the information in this book for yourself,
which is your constitutional right, the author and the publisher assume no responsibility for your actions.

Any people depicted in stock imagery provided by Thinkstock are models,
and such images are being used for illustrative purposes only.
Certain stock imagery © Thinkstock.

Printed in the United States of America.

ISBN: 978-1-4525-9442-2 (sc)
ISBN: 978-1-4525-9443-9 (e)

Library of Congress Control Number: 2014904846

Balboa Press rev. date: 3/28/2014

This book is dedicated to Jansje, my partner for a lifetime; my guardian angel who protects, guides and inspires me to share this knowledge with all of you. She is my gatekeeper and often the conduit for new beginnings. She is my source of inspiration to align myself with my authentic self and follow my inner guidance, our inner wisdom to become a fuller person.

This book is about our purpose in life. Through understanding of these issues you can achieve individual and collective growth and wellbeing.

Discovering: Who am I or: Who we are?

Thank you Jansje.

Foreword

**By–Daryl Wright. Managing Director: Bond Street One Eighty,
Corporate Renewal Specialist at Melbourne - Australia**

As a professional in organizational development I read many books about organizational change, leadership cultures, strategy and decision-making. Occasionally I encounter a book that inspires because it is written with a soul, because it is connecting views that were separated before. It offers new ways of thinking, new perceptions. This book "The Ego's Echo" is such a remarkable book in which an abundance of well-considered practical stories and new understandings lead to new knowledge, innovation and practice. The book is creative and special - it truly inspires.

I am impressed by Willem's new trinity of leadership model, his profiling tool to understand who you are, giving guidance to a become a fuller person. This book may play an important role in major transformational change on an individual and a collective level in organizations. It can even contribute to a scientific dialogue for people with an open mind, searching for consciousness and soul in the organization. It combines storytelling, sense making and creativity and, above all, you sense the passion for a life working together in harmony. An intriguing tool is Willem's road map for prosperity and sustainability. This in combination with the ULC diagnostic tool: "Perception table" what the individual's perceptions are of the situation the company finds themselves in. This book is a powerful instrument to form passionate teams working together in harmony for the better goods of the company.

Daryl, has more than twenty-five years of experience in the corporate renewal, business transformation and performance improvement industry. Daryl's focus is on the impact of Leadership on people.

****

Moboko: What surprises me the most...!!

"In my thirty-year career in human resources, I have come across a number of initiatives aimed at changing culture, influencing behavior, and motivating people.

What surprises me that most of the initiatives focused on what the organization can do and not necessarily on gaining the understanding of what the people think, it should be".

The stories and metaphors in this book are a testament to an organization tapping into people and connecting with each other to deliver value for the benefit of all. If you want to get the organization talking, allow space for listening without prejudice. In this way you are able to dig deep into the mine of human ability."

Moboko John Mahlaole, General manager human resources, Palabora Mining Company, SA.

Epigraph

Our conditioned fears, our false self, drive us to resist change. Unable to free ourselves of these emotional blockages, we succumb to them and chose to remain as we are. By surrendering to this conditioning from the past, this echo of the ego, we fail to discover our true being and what our authentic purpose in life is. We fail to "Awaken the Universe Within".

By learning how to harness our inner wisdom, to transcend our conditioned fears, our false self, we position ourselves to fully explore our true potential.

A roadmap to break these mental barriers is the ULC (Universal Life Cycle), a way to better understand others and ourselves. The ULC activates the spiral energy of our soul and our inner knowing. This positive spiral energy helps us to break through these barriers, giving us an understanding with which we can create an environment of trust and openness. Quality in man then unfolds.

When we recognize and understand how these positive and negative beliefs shape our behavior, we can use this knowledge to create flourishing physical lives filled with health, natural wealth and happiness. The ULC assists Individuals and Collectives (organizations) become aware of the steps to follow in the difficult process of letting go of the past, to create a new life in balance with all there is. Our inner knowing, our higher self, is this energy source, an unlimited source of positive energy. Through access to this source in the collective consciousness, we are able to create a new form of natural economy for humanity, with wellbeing for all of us.

To Awaken the "Universe Within" you focus on the interdependence of all, helping the individual to understand his or her relevance within the larger society and, in the search for "Who am I", help the individual to find one's own life purpose.

This book is about accessing your inner knowing, the source of inspiration and infinite energy. It is the energy of creation and the key to living in harmony. By guiding individuals in contributing towards a shared vision, according to their unique talents and strengths, we build a Collective in harmony. This requires an "Embracing Leadership" which respectfully, openly, and readily engages in dialogue with all, allowing each to voice their fears, encouraging their hopes and harvesting the wisdom required for activating higher levels of consciousness. The ULC, through interaction with art, provides the framework to assist in moving from the rational and thinking phase – Identity; through the heart and thought phase – Meaning - Who am I? to the Trinity in Leadership phase – Collective, where each individual is living a life filled with purpose, contributing according to their unique talents. Be aware and understand that you are born with the infinite energy of unconditional love, an invisible energy deep inside you - your inner knowing, the unique fingerprint of whom you really are. The power of openness is living in harmony with the environment and all there is.

Awaken the universe within.
Who am I?

Phil Connolly- Business consultant and editor's comment:

"Art speaks to us, in the words our soul chooses to hear. It is this unique relationship we have with art that de Liefde has leveraged in his Universal Life Cycle matrix, to allow us to express our inner selves, using art to mirror that which is within us, putting words to an understanding of our inner selves. Knowing our strengths and weaknesses, we can work on achieving our full potential. Under an embracing leadership this builds a collective where each individual; is supported in applying their greater strengths towards a common vision. The ULC provides a simple formula for this, whilst the many stories de Liefde relates are testimony as to how the ULC approach works in practice. This book represents a breakthrough in the quest for individual and collective fulfillment and harmony".

Contents

/ Go with the Flow

The Journey through Life

Do you live your life in complete freedom? Are you learning and growing in every moment? Is your dominant emotion one of joy? If you answered yes to these questions, then you are in alignment with your true self — you know whom you are and where you are going. You have shaken off the false beliefs acquired through your conditioning. You have greatly reduced fear within you. You have accessed your soul energy and, with it, the improved mental and spiritual health that you need for success on your journey through life. The moment we encounter that point where we profoundly realize that we are so much more than the limited physical creatures that

Go with the flow

society tells us we are, a new world of possibilities opens up. Indeed, we are spiritual beings having a physical experience, and every one of us has purpose, the fulfillment of which will bring us immense joy on our journey through life.

At a deep, subconscious level, we all know what our purpose is. Over time, the fear that we have accumulated through our societal conditioning has disconnected many of us from our source and the divine essence where our purpose is known. It blocks us from realizing the true genius that resides within us and from becoming the great icons that we are all capable of being. Few people have enough courage and belief in their authentic selves to transcend their conditioning and discover who they really are and what their true purpose is. Society demands that we live by the rules that are set for us. In response, our survival instinct has wired our natural conditioning to a habit of succeeding within that normative context, without questioning whether it really serves us as human beings in our core essence. Unfortunately however, when we ignore our core essence we lose our ability to live authentically, allowing depression, anger, and frustration to attach themselves as conditioners to our emotional and physical body. These lower-level emotions are our indicators that we have lost our direction in life and that it is time for us to rediscover the natural joy of living a life filled with purpose. To find our life of purpose, it is critical to reevaluate our individual as well as our collective context.

On a global scale we can see the damaging effect of inauthentic living, based on unhealthy leadership consciousness. In many cases, leaders of society have maintained power positions by pretending that they have "the knowing and the thinking" but, in reality, they are hiding their shortcomings by stigmatizing the collective through the creation and indoctrination of false beliefs and fear. This creates an energetic wound in society that we could call the "collective pain body", an energy that feeds frustration, anger, and depression. If we want to live our life from a domain of wholeness and in alignment with our purpose, we have to focus our attention on what it is we want in our own lives as individuals as well as in our relationship with the Collective. Fortunately, we are finally beginning to understand that the main conditioners preventing us from pursuing our true purpose in life and preventing us from rising to the true genius that resides within each one of us are fear, stigmatization and dogmatic social rules from the "knowing and thinking" authorities.

Once we have learned to invite our ego as a welcome natural partner and not as an opponent, we will discover who we really are and what our authentic life purpose is. With this awareness we can rediscover our wholeness, begin to live our lives authentically. We will become joyful again, filled with energy, enthusiasm, and the will to live our lives with passion and zest. We will learn to trust our profound intuition at all times and rely upon our inner knowing to guide us with ease through any obstacle that life throws at us.

In his book *The Biology of Belief*, Professor Bruce Lipton wrote the following:

> "I knew that if single cells are controlled by awareness of the environment, so too are we trillion-celled human beings. Just like a single cell, the character of our lives is determined not by our genes but by our responses to the environmental signals that propel life. There is no doubt that human beings have a great capacity for sticking to false beliefs …We are made in the image of God, and we need to put spirit back into the equation when we want to improve our physical and our mental health"

Lipton introduces in his book, the scientific evidence to show your genes do not control biology. He also introduces you to the exciting discoveries of *Epigenetics*, a new field of biology that is unraveling the mysteries of how the environment (nature) influences the behavior of cells without changing the genetic code. Positive thoughts have a profound effect on behavior and genes, but only when they are in harmony with subconscious programming. When we recognize how these positive and negative beliefs influence our biology, we can use this knowledge to create lives filled with health and happiness. He reveals why cells and people wanted to grow and how fear shuts down that growth.

Fear shutting down growth
Michel van Overbeeke

Carl Jung:
"Your vision will become clear only when you look into your heart. Who looks outside, dreams. Who looks inside, awakens."

Note: Be Aware!
When our senses are activated through the echo of the ego the result is often that the thinking mind creates fear, or an overruling desire for more matter, or lust for more power. The echo of the ego so often takes you away from your true self.

Story 1: The Ego's Echo versus Trust.

I was twenty years old and had just been appointed as an officer, sailing on a cargo ship on the Pacific Ocean between America and Asia. One night, I found myself on the bridge with the first officer. The sea had been stormy for days, and foam from the high waves crashed onto the deck with enormous force. We were sailing through waves thirty to fifty feet high. We were scared; the fear of not surviving was in the air. The first officer became increasingly nervous and eventually sent me to the captain's cabin. I was to bring him up onto the bridge immediately so that he, the captain, could take command again. In a state of agitation, I ran to the captain's cabin and knocked on his door. No reaction. I knocked again, harder this time, but once more there was no reaction. Eventually I opened the door and went over to the captain's bed. "I'm sorry to wake you, Captain," I said, "but the first officer asks if you'd come up onto the bridge because there's such a terrible storm."

The captain, who was still half asleep, gave me a penetrating look and answered that he had apprised himself of the weather situation before getting into his bunk, and until such time as he appeared on the bridge, there was no reason for anyone to be concerned. He went on to say that during his life as a captain, he had survived worse weather conditions. He was absolutely convinced that everything was under control, and he now wanted to go back to sleep. I was dumbstruck and mumbled, "Aye, aye, Captain," turned on my heel, and hurried back to the bridge.

I told the first officer what had happened. I had the impression that he was no longer in control of the situation. He said he had to go to the toilet. Suddenly I was the only responsible person on the bridge, and the ship continued to drift between the gigantic waves like a cockleshell. I waited in vain for the first officer to return. After I'd stood alone on the bridge for half an hour, bathed in sweat, an old experienced boatswain appeared with a pot of coffee. I assumed the captain had sent him to see if everything was all right.

"Just look at those magnificent waves," he shouted, "that's something you don't experience if you're an ordinary man sitting in your garden in Amsterdam!" He sat next to me, drank his cup of coffee, and then left. Once more I was alone, but something important had changed. I could feel that I had enough strength and confidence to cope with the situation, and a smile appeared on my face.

The Invitation

Albert Einstein is well known for his admiration of the rational mind and its incredible ability for complex logic and deep thinking. But, like a philosopher, he wondered a lot about life and the nature of being. One insight he expressed follows:

> "The intuitive mind is a sacred gift and the rational mind is a faithful servant.
> We have created a society that honors the servant and has forgotten the gift".

Have we lost the miracle of life, our natural ability to be in tune with the subtle whisper in which life expresses its magnificent wisdom and showers us with its continuous flow of beauty and abundance? Where there should be unity and connection, we have division in diversity. The "I" has made it separate from the "We", to which it owes its existence. In turn the "We" has often sought to make a number of the unique "I". Emotionally, mentally, physically, politically, economically, socially and environmentally we find imbalance and disconnection in the "I" and the "We", as well as in our soul. The global economic crisis, natural disasters, and sociopolitical uprisings are just a few of the indicators that systems are collapsing. In many shapes and forms, voices for a new consciousness give rise to a global intuitive awareness of a need for fundamental change and transformation.

The biggest challenge for the industrial/technological, rational driven world is that we have lost identity (disconnect of self) and meaning (disconnect of purpose) in life by enslaving ourselves to the relentless and endless pursuit to produce material economic growth, resulting in a total disintegration of the natural balance of life. If we look to all of these problems — and there are many — we can ask the question, "Can they be solved?"

The answer is "Yes." What is needed is more understanding of the miracle of life, and a lifestyle of wellbeing for all. Each person, within the context of the collective, needs to "Awaken the Universe Within".

To intuitively reconnect with the essence of life, it is critical that we again become aware of our existential life journey and that we reconnect with our authentic selves, as it is in that connection that our life pulse originates. While the detail may be complex, the principle is just unconditional love. We need more heart/soul energy in every aspect of daily life. Heart, in its earthbound flow, is the love and affective connection, the essence of emotional intelligence. The heart's energy is the soul of your inner knowing. The miracle of life is that if we find balance, if we are able to embrace our connection with all of life's essence we can all enjoy the unlimited prosperity that is the inextricable result of soul and matter integration. To recognize the universal flow of life and to connect both individually and collectively in a manner that is in harmonious alignment with your personal being and the collective development potential, is the main purpose of the Universal Life Cycle. Through its art, a journey of boundless possibilities of soul/matter manifestations opens up and can connect us with our inner wisdom.

I invite you on this ULC journey through life, the not expected dialogue.

2 Meeting Jan Montyn

The Request

I met the artist Jan Montyn in 1992 and shared with him my vision on leadership. I presented my thoughts to him as follows:

> Trust people deeply; choose to approach life from a state of unconditional love; believe strongly in the "we" and in the healing power of positive energy; be consistently courageous in putting the truth on the table; and approach difficult situations by entering into dialogue with the entire organization.

My famous slogan was " If your intentions are sincere then the universe will help you naturally". Not knowing then that it was an awareness cry, for the belief in the interconnection of science and the spiral thought energy of the universe. My experience was that the universe helps if your intentions are sincere, solutions and ideas seemingly come from nowhere. Believe that you are able to liberate yourself from the problem or issue at that specific moment in time, and create space in your subconscious mind.

I asked Jan if he could make a few etchings of my thoughts. Jan Monty's answer was simply "yes I could".

The Result

Jan went away, and, exactly nine months later, he came back to me with nine images engraved on plates, the nine etches and eighteen prints, the etchings.

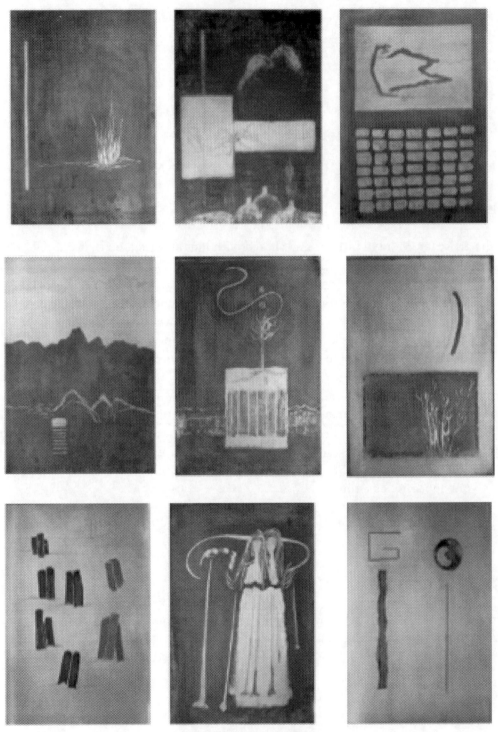

Nine-Etch plates by Jan Montyn

"I only created etching images; gave them a title reflecting your thoughts," were Jan's simple words. "You know the deeper reality and meaning behind the physical form of this art. It's up to you." Jan gave the etches and etchings specific sequences. The nine etches he called the metamorphose and the sequences of the eighteen etchings, and the trinity of the twenty-seven, the energy flows.

Jan was able to make my thoughts visually tangible by feeling my vision, listening to my stories, and capturing my simple sentences (trust people deeply, etc.). Later on I called the nine etched plates the ULC (Universal Life Cycle). For me, the plate's energy holds the source code that became the DNA for the series of eighteen prints (etchings) made from those nine etching plates.

It was in 1993 that Jan presented me with the nine etching plates. To understand the potential of the original thought that sparked it all, has taken me eighteen years. My first book was completed in 2002, and the second was published in 2011—two cycles of nine years. But then a new thought emerged. Could this art, that I have called the ULC, be used as an instrument to look at individuals or organizations that are out of balance? The thought developed, uncovering a new dimension of perception/feeling embedded in three phases; the rational and thinking phase — Identity, Meaning and the Collective Phase. A new cycle of the ULC journey began.

Reflecting on this journey, the rational mind might ask, "How is it possible that the worlds of two people who were relative strangers, arrived at the same point at the same time with such significant insight? For me, this is where thinking reaches its limits, confined as it is to the material world. The only way to truly understand this phenomenon of synchronicity is to observe it from the heart, to feel it by having the experience of being one with the spirit of infinity. The universe can then bring that insight to you; it knows you need it and knows you are ready to receive it in that exact moment.

In order to manifest thought into reality, you need an encounter with another person who can see and receive the thought. It is in the transference of energy that meaning emerges and miracles happen. True artists know and recognize that process, as do those who see leadership as a precious calling. Jan's gift was the understanding of the thought. Through feeling and imagination, he was able to represent this in art. It gave vital impetus to the development of the ULC. Therefore, it is not only mine; its identity radiates the spirit of Jan, who made it visibly tangible, and Jansje, who was always prepared to listen to my ideas — and was not scared to challenge them — and who always encouraged me to externalize my spirit through sharing my journey of insight and discovery with you. It is important for me to acknowledge that many people have shared this journey with me. Each one has contributed a unique way of observing, participating, and sharing wisdom and understanding. These insights have unlocked more of the ULC's secrets and have deepened the collective understanding of the ULC.

The Role of Art in the ULC

The name Universal Life Cycle came as a thought for a diagnostic tool—the feeling was that it was universal. The titles of the art brought me to the three phases of a trinity: Identity, Meaning, and Collective. The twenty-seven images represent infinite spiral energy; an invitation to see, feel and explore. In the center column are the nine etches, the source. On the left and right are the eighteen etchings. See front cover columns The trinity of the ULC and the twenty-seven images

Question:
Can the ULC be instrumental in "Who am I?"

The answer is Yes. *In the ULC process of "who you are", the etch plates function as mirrors of recognition for the soul's inner knowing. Be open minded to experience the ULC's universal message. It is the unknown of the not expected that can give you a sense of feeling for the ULC's potential to assist you in becoming a fuller person. It assists in the development of a more harmonious society. This creative process makes it possible for us to connect with our inner knowing, soul and intuition. Art helps us to connect with our reservoir of unlimited infinite energy, the energy of creation, which is not conditioned by fear and therefore can manifest more successfully.*

In 'Spiral Dynamics' written by D.E Beck and Ch. C Cowan they write: "In his book '*Cycles*' Samuel A Schreiner, Jr., invite the reader to discover 'Cycleland' claiming that 'cycles are at work everywhere and in everything. It is more than a possibility that the study of cycles will one day reveal the long-sought-after unifying principle that will enable man to understand how the universe really works."

The Universal Life Cycle uses art to engage our conscious awareness and our inner-knowing state of awareness, opening up space for authentic wisdom to arise. By allowing ourselves to be transported by the imagination of the art, we are invited to create a new feeling about our own situation and to reflect on our own specific perceptions. In this way, art can cast doubt on our often unthinkingly accepted interpretations of reality and our methods of seeing and reasoning.

Using art in transformation processes offers several advantages over more rational management and consultancy approaches. Art has a strong emotional appeal—it elicits a response and can provoke one without expecting a particular reaction. Art does not enter our process of giving meaning. Art creates space because it leaves the interpretation up to us.

In the words of Alfred Barr, Jr., the first curator of the Museum of Modern Art in New York; above all, art is "an invitation to see."

1)mind logic   2)spirit flow   3)heart feeling

The trinity of the ULC and the twenty-seven images

Art can present us with mysteries, logical inconsistencies, or optical illusions without intending to embarrass us and without giving the impression of concealing solutions. In this way, art can stimulate us without being patronizing. Art facilitates the decision- making by the leader in a natural-open atmosphere. Art honors the members of a collective(company) to voice their voices on the different situations.

Belgian artist René Magritte, said his paintings were an invitation to "experience problems" and to open minds to "the mystery/the unknown." Art can be symbolic and abstract without being concerned with whether we find it recognizable, useful, or sound. In this way, art offers a universal language and a hidden message and, above all, an invitation to see and feel.

Organizations are living organisms. They, like humans, have a soul, a collective soul.

3 Evolution of the Universal Life Cycle

The Origins

Always the challenge was to capture "the thought and the feeling" in words. In this sense, the feeling and inner knowing were always light-years ahead of the plodding, rational mind. The inner knowing was the guide, the light at the end of the tunnel. My first book, Lekgotla: *The Art of Leadership through Dialogue*, focused on the collective, explaining the power of using the wisdom of the crowd.

Dr. Maki Mandela wrote the following passage in that book:

> This book is a meeting of souls from Africa and Europe in an attempt to find common ground. It is written for family, friends, colleagues known and unknown, for those who find themselves at the crossroads of their lives or their careers, and for those who are searching and yearning for a source of change. It is for those who are willing to dig deeper, to look beyond the surface of things. It is an invitation to all to learn from a lekgotla as a continuing journey into the future—one driven by caring and commitment to common ground.

The book was based on the understanding of the principle "I am because we are": the awareness of the connection between and interdependence of all things. I believe that dialogue or communication is the only way that a collective can remain healthy, focused, and united. When people are denied the right to speak and be heard, they lose a sense of belonging (identity), which creates disconnection (meaning) and ultimately a weaker whole (collective).

In the second book, *ULC: The Leadership Navigator: Governance without Fear*, the focus shifted to the individual inside of the collective and how the ego can act as a force on and within the collective, showing how ego, the "I," has become the dominant mode of leadership in much of the world today. It highlighted how such leadership relies on energies such as fear, force, and dominance to have its way. The ULC was developed as a tool to help nurture better models of leadership, to

13

have the "I" work better in the context of the "We" in pursuit of outcomes that are beneficial to all, which is called "embracing leadership." What blocks our growth to becoming a fuller person as human beings is our conditioning. It limits our full potential. When the "I" and the "We" are unified in harmony, the energy in passion and motivation is abundant, and prosperity is the result.

In *ULC: The Leadership Navigator,* Professor van der Merwe described it as follows:

> "Willem de Liefde took an age-old African concept and constructed an ingenious matrix he calls the Universal Life Cycle (ULC) to help you understand yourself, your team, and your company. This understanding sets the phase for dialogue (LeKgotla), creates an environment in which positive change can take place, and assists in the process of letting go of the past. The ULC is a clever tool to help carry your company through the difficult process of awareness, reconciliation, and forgiveness. This process leads to the realization that our success lies in working together in harmony to become a WE driven organization, thus moving toward an African Ubuntu approach".

This third book represents a further step in the evolution of this work, its maturation. The focus is now on how the individual and the collective are intertwined, how there needs to be balance with all there is. If the individual becomes a fuller person, then this self will ultimately have an impact on the collective. This is a journey toward knowing who you are as an individual and what your purpose or essence is in this life, knowing and accepting yourself.

Phases I, II and III	Titles of the ULC nine intersections ULC etches - The source images		
I. Identity	1 Not expected	2 Encounter	3 Transformation
II. Meaning	4 Movement	5 Enlightenment	6 Liberation
III. Collective	7 Community	8 Embracement	9 Full ending

A matrix is an environment or material in which something develops, or the place in or from which, form originates. This idea or concept has been used in many different contexts, in both theory and practice, and has been adopted by many cultures. It is a useful framework to begin understanding the Universal Life Cycle. For now, let us keep our focus on the three phases as they relate to the nine images that make up the complete cycle. Each of the nine images represents a life intersection that involves transformation of energy, critical in harnessing the continual flow toward the next life intersection. The diagnostic power of the nine themes is unexpectedly powerful and pure, and can bring about an enormous acceleration and awareness in finding solutions for a particular situation or issue.

The ULC etches are also used as the source code from which individuals make selections which reflect the soul, the dream, the inner knowing, and the inner desire; recognize the inner truth in the self, and see if the mental, spiritual and emotional energies are in balance; and assist in understanding the self and the other person better (when done in a collective setting).

The eighteen etchings are used for finding the talents; the practical, emotional, and mental skills; and the pitfalls and the conditioners acquired through false beliefs. The etchings also mirror the skills available in a team to align the individual talents, feelings, and inner desires.

The ULC profiling tool can be used to compose combinations of employees across different departments in a line organization, moving them toward working together to solve complex unexpected situations or to develop new thoughts and ideas that can then move the organization or society forward. The complex line/matrix structure of organizations is an obstacle to soft, tangible spiral energy that can make teams work well together. The culture of building *silos* (different individuals or camps) and the energy of "I am the best" do not facilitate the flow of spiral energy. Analyzing the Identity, Meaning, and Collective alignment of an organization can give a diagnosis of the strength or the weakness of the collective feeling about identity and meaning. By using the ULC in a corporate, the response is not aimed at a specific person or department but at the organization as a whole. It is a picture of the motivation/passion of the employees, the strength and the weakness of internal communication of the understanding of the vision. It is not threatening but rather gives people relief; it places their truth on the table. This will be explained in Chapter 11 as the ULC perception table.

> "The observations that are not explainable by current scientific theories are the most valuable, for they may propel the field forward in the next cycle of innovation, possibly to a paradigm shift".
> By D. L. Jewett, in "What's Wrong With Single Hypotheses"

So, what is most needed? Balance. By this I mean realigning the energy of the mind with the energy of the heart. It is the power of the individual inside the collective and, inverted, the impact of the collective on the individual. Such an interface, interdependency, does not conform to the logic of opposites; instead it is about two mirroring parts that, aligned, make a complete whole. This is polarity, an energy flow from A to B and back, inside of a cycle, repeated infinitely. The true spark of wisdom is not knowledge but thought. Thought is always adaptable to change. The most prosperous and sustainable natural organizations are those that adapt to change without losing the fundamental identity that is the heart of their fertility. But identity alone is not enough. There must be feeling to give it meaning. Meaning is the force underlying any human interaction — family, community, society, or business. A collective that has a strong identity that is meaningful, is able to work in harmony toward achieving the common goal. Without identity, one cannot give meaning to life. Without meaning in life, one cannot create a harmonious or prosperous sustainable collective/society.

The ULC is about:

- The continuity of existence of humanity through time.
- Reigniting awareness and positive energy.
- Aligning your conscious- with your subconscious mind.
- Profiling: Who am I
- Unlocking your inner knowing.

This process is about individuals stepping into their individual power and taking absolute responsibility for themselves and their lives. Moving beyond blame and anger towards acceptance and empowerment of the self by taking full control of all aspects of their lives. When we give away our power or give up responsibility, we are not fully in control of our presence in our lives.

Identity is the foundation for sustainability, the platform nourishing the fertile soil for the meaning of a healthy collective. Looking to nature, it is the roots of plants and trees that sustain their lives. If the roots of a collective, our identity, are not healthy, the organization is not flourishing. Signs of this may be stress, no joy, gossiping, demotivation, bad communication, and so on.

Achieving Balance

We can come back into balance through an awareness of the interdependency within and between the individual and the collective. The individual supports the development of a healthy collective through sharing their unique skills and talents with the collective and having the collective support for the development of a healthy individual. The basis of this is an understanding of the need to bring the heart and mind back into alignment.

What is key to this alignment is the spiral energy, the energy flow between mind and heart (soul). The image of polarity came as the solution: attraction rather than opposition. Polarity, heart and mind united in spiral energy. Like the north and south poles, which have a magnetic energy field between them. That trinity, as a unity, is very useful to us for navigation on Earth. If we see only opposition, we separate ourselves. We create boundaries between others and ourselves. In separating, we lose touch with the balance in the self. This is the tragedy of duality. We exist in a world of polarity but have, as humans, turned our back on its divine logic, those natural laws that order the universe of matter. Polarity is the very glue that holds it all together. The madness of the modern human's world is duality, the belief that everything can be explained or solved by science and technology or dogmatic religion and fear. Polarity is the marriage of the two forms of consciousness, "I think, therefore I am" and "I am, because we are."

The individual journey to becoming a fuller person is then a mirror of the same journey within the collective. If the individual is out of balance, then so is the collective, but when in balance, the individual and collective can create form and sustainability, which is about well-being for all, a reconnection to wholeness. In the Old Testament and Koran we also find the wisdom and the words "I am that I am."

The Universal Life Cycle represents the dance of infinity between the "I" and the "We", to manifest "I am that I am". It represents the 'I' embracing the 'We' and the 'We' embracing the 'I.' Maintaining the culture of a We society requires continuous awareness of this dance of infinity between our ego, our soul, and the collective soul; continuously understanding the dynamics between the diverse individual and the collective energy in the intersections of the Universal Life Cycle.

The process represented above is the universal, invisible spiral energy flow between the phases and the nine intersections. Later it will be explained in more depth. This is an ideal picture of when there are no blockages or imbalances anywhere. Importantly, this matrix speaks to both the individual and collective equally; in fact, it does not even hold them to be separate. Think of any collective, be it a government, company, organization, club, family or marriage. When a problem emerges, the Not expected, a positive or negative event taking the community/ organization or individual by surprise (this might be political instability, a loss in market share, or a crisis in leadership), the outcome depends entirely on the response of the individuals inside the collective. Are they stuck in fear to survive (the echo of the ego) or able to free themselves from the past?

What has been surprising, working with management teams, is that there is little or no fear of the individual opening him or her self, in the belief it is in the interest of the team or the organization's wellbeing. Honestly expressing who they are to one another, inside the collective setting, people naturally wanted to and are enlightened by sharing the truth of themselves with others. Think about this for a second, speaking freely without fear, inside a corporate setting. It is certainly not the norm, but the impact is profound.

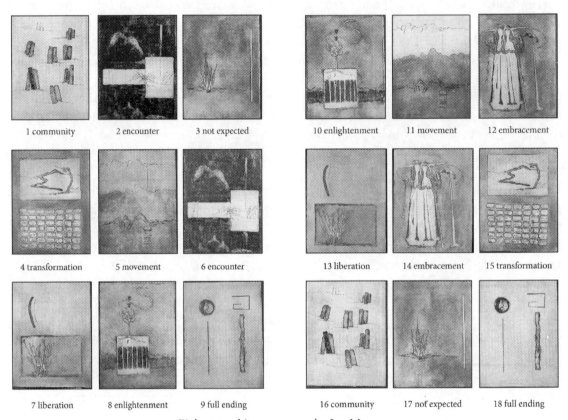

| 1 community | 2 encounter | 3 not expected | | 10 enlightenment | 11 movement | 12 embracement |

| 4 transformation | 5 movement | 6 encounter | | 13 liberation | 14 embracement | 15 transformation |

| 7 liberation | 8 enlightenment | 9 full ending | | 16 community | 17 not expected | 18 full ending |

Eighteen etchings sequence by Jan Montyn

Story 2: "We" Embracing the "I" speaking freely

The CEO who, in his own words, during the day felt like "taking a blunt axe to myself and to this business," invited the executives to a workshop. This newly formed team was not performing well as a collective. The CEO felt that a whole new direction was needed.

Prior to the workshop, each individual had a one-on-one ULC profiling interview, based on the images they selected. This allowed the building of a profile of each person; identifying his or her unique talents and abilities as well as their pitfalls or blockages/conditioners. The executives also selected an etch reflecting the company's problems. By doing this, we were able to create a profiling map of both the individual and collective. On the day of the session, there was some hesitancy and looks of disbelief on the faces of the executives. As individuals, they were asked to take a large piece of paper, find a place on the floor, and, with pieces of charcoal, draw what each person felt was the company's problem and what could be the solution to that problem. Some hours later, already tired of being made to sit on the floor, they were further challenged to stop drawing from the mind, the perspective of the business, and to capture the flow of spiritual energy as it related to the beauty of life and working as a team—in short, drawing from the heart! Looking at them, one could imagine their thoughts: *Oh, he has lost it now. Bringing us here to draw, talk about hearts. What is this going to do to change our situation?*

However, they continued, many of them making some real changes to what they had initially rendered. Toward the end of the day, the group came together in the lekgotla, where each one was asked to explain what he or she had drawn.

The purpose of the drawing was to allow each individual to come in dialogue internally and then share that unique insight with the group. The individual process is often reflective of the collective one, and so the personal dialogue feeds into a bigger group conversation in an environment of trust and sharing of truth.

The first executive to present had spent close to an hour, eyes locked, fixated on the mass of glass windows running along the length of one side of the venue. The view looked out over, symbolically, the cradle of humankind: trees, bushes, and grassland, rolling hills, grazing wildlife, and a cacophony of birds playing nature's soundtrack. He had disappeared into this world before he made a single mark on his paper. He explained: "My initial approach to this was from the head side. This is something I am told I do too often."

In synchronizing with the nature of the cradle of human kind, his heart opens. His initial drawing was a mixture of rational statements and images as well as a few metaphorical drawings that spoke to them. The final drawing was quite different. And when he spoke, there was really a sense that he had touched on something deep and profound. His words reflected this, and they accurately captured the company's current blockages, something that would be expressed in even more detail by the group over the rest of the day. Slowly he found his voice. When he started to speak, he really came alive. He came to talk about the heart that we had asked them to draw. He really reflected—to himself, his colleagues, and the company—what the challenge was. It was as if he had found the power of a Messenger. Interestingly, these talents of a Messenger were the ones we had identified as one of his unique gifts to the company and a key drive in their efforts to change. He said, "I didn't want to draw a heart because they (our people) have got the heart; they are part of our company's heart; it's about purpose and people coming to work for a reason."

There was a knowing within that group, which came out strongly during the workshop. They all could recognize that the problem was both within themselves as individuals as well as in the company; they were intertwined. The range of difficulties were manifesting at both personal and professional levels. The overriding message that came out of the workshop, expressed by the entire team, was that they needed more heart energy. They had lost it. How were they going to get it back? This team could become a winning team if they opened up and exposed themselves to the other persons and to their employees.

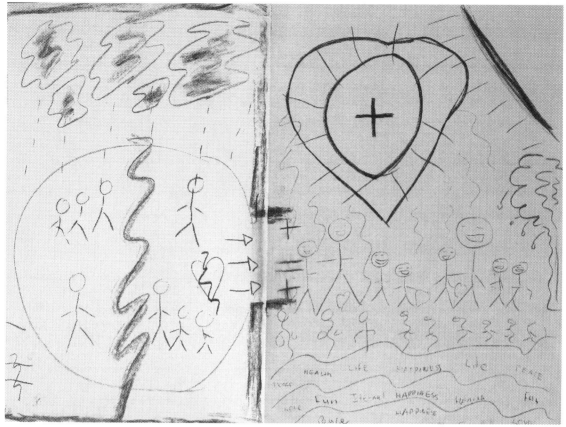

More heart

The Next Evolution

Polarity is the logic that orders the world of matter and spirit. It has, for many people, the illusion of being similar to duality. But it is actually the infinite energy flow of our spirit in matter. It is the energy flow between the mind (logic) and the heart (feeling), not as opponents but as partners in diversity. Polarity, then, operates cyclically. Be aware that duality operates contra productive or even destructive.

Individuals and collectives are dynamic, living entities. Polarity works in the service of harmony inside diversity, while duality seeks to fashion the world and to assert uniformity through control, therefore creating illness. Become a source of positive energy; let the light inside you shine outside.

The nine intersections of the ULC could serve as a metaphor for all the phases and energy cycles we go through in life to find our purpose. We move through these steps in cycles, repeatedly, in the physical world. The moment of conception is the spark of new life. Individual lives come together inside of a pairing. Both possess the necessary biology to perform this act. But this explanation alone does not seem sufficient to describe what we call the "miracle of life". If we look beyond the realms of science, religion and philosophy, past the ability of comprehension, we will see what is at work here.

The Miracle of Life

The miracle is one and one combining in creation. Male and female come together to perform an act of unity. Infinity meets matter as two lives become one. The act of creation is a divine energy, and so, in that moment, two physical bodies, them selves created by the same energy, connect to the source. The source is everything, and everything is the source; it is the beginning and end, the cycle. This is the wisdom of unity, the infinite. Two together, of both matter and spirit, become one through a process which is the sum and more than them. Trinity. The magic begins. From here, the journey of life, of a new life, begins. Traveling through nine phases, or months, to birth, every being must also pass successfully through three important phases: Identity, Meaning, and Collective.

From infinity, the invisible, the universe or source, comes mind. It is the starting point for the physical body. The bonded sperm and egg are already matter, but more is needed for life. The subconscious matter memory of the cells (invisible), together with the dividing cells (physical matter) begin the process of imprinting what is needed to create a foundation, giving form (creation) to a new life's identity. The first three months pass. But there are more ingredients to complete this story. The cells set about creating a nest, building a new home for its partner, the soul. This is a very necessary element to creating a whole—a functional being. The soul arrives in the home of its partner, the mind and heart. The energy of the soul is needed for life; without significance or purpose, can there be such a thing as life? This is meaning. And so three more months pass.

Importantly, the soul arrives with its inner knowing and desire. Souls, like minds, have presented themselves to the world of matter in numbers unimaginable. But the soul's inner knowing is unique. The soul then, is the blueprint for that life, its unique purpose. The two lover's souls and mind, united in identity and meaning, must now make manifest. For if two spirits, dancing inside, burning passion for one another do not realize their love, then it is but a thought or a feeling without a home, an identity without meaning or meaning searching for identity. They must balance this in reality. Let us call this the *collective*.

Inside the process of manifesting, mind and soul are one inside matter. These two invisible energies, having come from source, must marry inside the physical if they are to be able to express themselves in the material world. This is the last three months, the full maturation of the happenings of the tangible material and intangible spiritual worlds. It is collective, because it is many different things coming together as one. Things easily explained marry/bind with those impossibly indescribable and vice versa, needing one another to be whole. In the miracle of birth, with the first breath the spirit spiral energy arrives, activating the thinking of the mind and inner knowing of the soul, with its infinite thought potential to awaken the universe within you; the feeling heart, our conscious knowing in matter, and our subconscious inner knowing in soul. The feeling heart is the sensing precision radar of the soul to inform a person if something is right or wrong.

The nine phases of the ULC, including the artwork that is used as the symbol of each one, are the processes of coming to life, the merging of the material and spiritual world. A short description follows of what happens at the level of the material and spiritual worlds in the nine steps of coming into physical life. Each phase represents one of the nine months that we are in the womb on our journey to life in the physical world. The marriage of the art with the words is key to the ULC. If we spoke only to the thinking part of us in words, we would just talk to the mind; instead, the art is there to speak to the feeling part of us, the heart, as well as to our inner knowing and inner desire — the domain of infinity and intuition.

These nine intersections naturally occur in three phases: Identity, Meaning, and Collective.

ULC and the miracle of life

Unconditional love

Phase I: Identity note phase 1 together on a page

1. **Not Expected**

   At the moment of conception, the sperm of the biological father fertilizes the egg in the uterus of the mother. Of over 180 million sperm, only one will make it through to impregnate an egg. Two cells, one with female energy and one with male, become one cell. From this unity, they begin to multiply into identical cells: one becomes two, two become four, four become eight, and so on. In each one, there is the identical cellular memory, mind. The wonder begins. This is the Not expected, which will always have a profound impact on the lives of all involved. This is thought where wisdom starts.

2. **Encounter**

    There is an energetic bond and dialogue between identical cells as they continue multiplying, building the foundation of the new home for the soul. The cellular memory carries the memory of survival and infinite wisdom needed for life in the physical world. This cell's memory in physical matter is an unbroken, physical chain reaching back billions of years to the beginning of life on earth. During this phase, the embryo is formed, and as the cells continue to multiply, each one knows its final destination and what part and function of the physical body it will become, "understanding, activating the senses."

3. **Transformation**

    During transformation cells that were previously identical start to differentiate, moving away from one whole toward growing into their unique functions; heart, lungs, spine, brain, liver, etc. The embryo is starting to become a fetus. If this dialogue phase does not feel right, this is where miscarriage generally occurs as the infinite energy is not there to support this life (a barrier). At the end of this phase the heart cells start contracting, called beating. The identity of the new individual is given its physical form.

Phase II: Meaning

4. **Movement**

    The fetus begins to physically move. This is triggered by brain cells, which send signals to the different parts of the developing body in preparation for life in the physical world. The organs, except for the lungs, start to function. Some of the senses of the fetus are activated. The new life starts to become meaningful to it self. The mother begins to feel the child and becomes aware of something unique inside of her, "the mercy feeling."

5. **Enlightenment**

    At this phase, the mind, in matter, has created a physical home for the soul. The fetus is fully developed in the sense that everything that is needed to become a fully functioning physical body is there; what is left now is just to grow. Enlightenment is an important meaning-making phase, as the fetus also takes on its sex, its male or female judgment of the self. For example, if it is a female, the fetus will develop five million egg cells in the ovary, all of which she will have available in her entire lifetime; this is the "abundance of life," even though only around five hundred of these will become potentially fertile.

So there is meaning making at the level of biology as well as at the level of self. When the new physical home is ready, the soul will arrive. The soul arrives with her infinite conscious with her inner knowing and desire, the unique purpose for this life, our unique fingerprint. The physical fetus and soul are now one; everything is present as two entities are living together. Soul is the carrier of infinite matter, an invisible energy.

6. **Liberation**
   The fetus is beginning to live in polarity with the mother; they are both unique but live as one. The fetus now only needs the mother for feeding and to pump the baby's blood, which carries its oxygen and food. The rest of the fetus's functions are now its own. For example, the fetus is able to digest and process nutrients and excrete its own waste. The fetus is becoming liberated physically as well, in the way that it is now a distinct, meaningful being, beauty.

Phase III: Collective

7. **Community**
   The fetus starts to sense the outside world, to see light, hear sounds, etc. This has the impact of creating perception of the bigger environment (community). The fetus' senses begin to perceive that it is part of something, a collective that is bigger than itself.

8. **Embracement**
   The fetus now becomes a baby. It is fully developed, and its senses are now activated. At this point, the mother embraces the baby by giving it an extra dose of anti-bodies, far more than before, which the baby will need to protect itself against bacteria, viruses, and other potential threats as its own immune system develops. This extra protection is an act of both biology and unconditional love, a physical and emotional connection. In this phase, the baby, physically, is in control of itself as a separate entity from the mother, an individual, ready for birth and life in the physical world. It has the foundation of "we".

9. **Full ending**
   The ninth state is birth. The spirit arrives at the moment of the first breath. The lungs, until now, have been inactive. For the first time, the heart pumps blood to the lungs which returns oxygenated; previously the blood from the heart had bypassed the lungs. This activates the baby's unique journey and purpose in life starts. The spirit's invisible energy flows between lungs and heart, our soul in physical matter, our heart activates the subconscious and conscious mind in the brain to manifest in the physical world. The process of thinking and physical action to manifest in the self; the world starts. The soul transmutes Universal energy into (physical matter) heart energy, needed for

aligning the conscious and subconscious mind in the baby. The birth is the end and a new beginning. The newborn is now a collective in its physical self as well as within the bigger world.

The wisdom of the cycle is eternal, a circle that has no start or finish. The "not expected" is the full ending; the beginning is the end, and the end is the beginning. The cycle is an unbroken energy field that is present everywhere in the universe. So inside of the journey to life, the marriage of matter and spirit in our physical body, we find a universal model that can help us understand life in practice. This is the recognition of the inner truth within the self, when the mental, spiritual, and emotional energies are balanced in harmony.

"The Western mindset places a greater emphasis on the "I," the healing of the individual, whereas we Africans believe that if the community is healed, we as individuals are healed in the process." by *Lemaseya Khama - Gaborone, Botswana.* Let us go from illness to wellness. Enjoying the miracle of life.

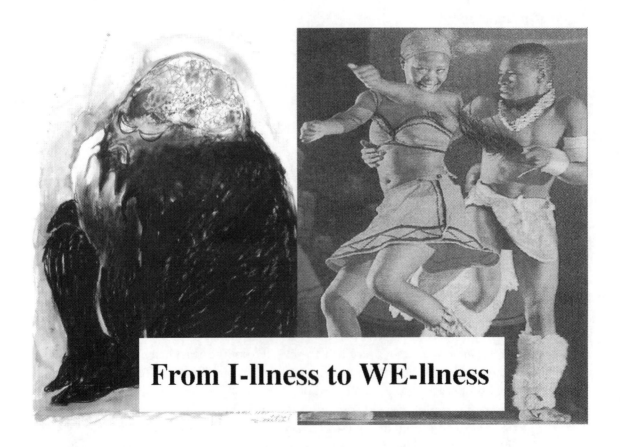

From I-llness to WE-llness

Universal Life Cycle Overview

By extension then, the nine steps and three phases, Identity, Meaning and Collective, apply not only to the individual but also to every collective. The ULC then, is something that can be used by any individual or collective; these nine steps are so deeply a part of our being that they are relevant in all areas or spheres of human personal or social life. If there is no identity, it is not possible to give meaning, and without meaning the building of strong collectives is unattainable. Great leaders, we could say, are experts in the "birthing" process, creating new forms for a sustainable future.

Deepak Chopra stated this idea in the following way:

> "Every time you are tempted to react in the same old way, ask if you want to be a prisoner of the past or a pioneer of the future".

The Three Phases

What follows is an overview of the life-cycle model and the benefits it can bring, based on situational analysis. The model reflects how we pass through the phases and intersections of the ULC and characterizes the social dynamic that goes with it. Participants identify with specific phases of the cycle during a situational analysis. All the illustrations in this book are used as metaphors, representations of reality, through which a process of free association and emotional involvement is stimulated. The illustrations are used as metaphors, representations of reality, through which a process of free association and emotional involvement is stimulated.

ULC is unlocking a person's power of a thought, appeared in someone's imagination, but the ability to visualize our thought is often one of our least understood mental and emotional powers.

The three phases of the ULC

Identity
Meaning
Collective,

are the roadmap for the way forward. If there are unresolved problems or barriers they are solved in this natural process of identification and awareness of the situation.

The Universal Life Cycle - "An invitation to see"

Phases I, II and III	Titles of the nine intersections Of the ULC		
I. Identity	1 Not expected Thought to *Wisdom*	2 Encounter Senses to *Understanding*	3 Transformation Awareness to *Knowledge*
II. Meaning	4 Movement Feeling to *Mercy*	5 Enlightenment Reconciliation to *Judgment*	6 Liberation Forgiveness to *Beauty*
III. Collective	7 Community Manifest to *Eternity*	8 Embracement We to *Foundation*	9 Full ending Abundance to *Kingdom*

At the first phase of identity formation, the emphasis is on creating self-consciousness. Making sense and restoring self-confidence are major themes of identity development and maintenance. The power of the thought is the spark restoring the self-confidence in our emotional and mental power. During the second phase meaning is strengthened and people are inspired to accept and implement new concepts. In the third phase, shared meaning is transformed into a forceful individual or community with a strong externally directed energy.

It is in the third phase that enduring individual or community success can become the breeding ground for complacency and or arrogance. As a consequence, external feedback will be neglected and the community will get more and more isolated and alienated from the environment. In such a situation, the strong individual or community is no longer an advantage. The closed character and the binding force of the individual or community results in a strong, internally-orientated culture, and the development of a defensive strategy. This strengthens the alienated position of the collective and they feel threatened. These threats reinforce the already existing cultural "separation" of the community's defensive or dominating strategy. The collective's development process spirals down to the phase at which identity is threatened at first and, ultimately, is lost.

One can only break the negative spiral by starting a dialogue, an encounter in a new way, with members of the wider community, creating awareness of the situation they are in. This allows people to meet one another in different ways. A breakthrough will not be realized unless the members of the organization are helped to face reality in a social setting they are not familiar with. At the end of the dialogue, the leader has to take a decisive autocratic decision. That's what people are expecting from the embracing leader.

The process represented above is a universal, invisible spiral energy flow between the phases and the nine intersections. This is an ideal picture where there are no blockages or imbalances anywhere. Importantly, this matrix speaks to both the individual and collective equally, in fact it does not even hold them to be separate.

The ULC initiates the proactive process of awareness through which subconscious knowledge, your inner knowing, will be linked to conscious knowing. (Logic and thinking) This creates an interaction between objective and subjective knowledge. The power of thought is infinite.

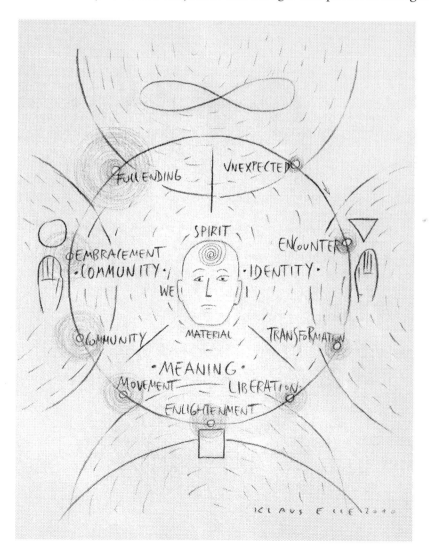

ULC's - Proactive process flow through: Identity – Meaning and Collective phases

Phases I-II-III	The Nine Intersections
I -Identity	1 **Not expected**, a not expected event, fear for the future, confusion, need for thought, a new form, vision. 2 **Encounter**, open dialogue, every voice is heard internally and externally. Sharing the truth and goals, listen to people's fear. Dialogue to sense people's feeling about the new vision (form) and next phase. 3 **Transformation**, creation of a new form and strengthening of the identity. Formulating the new goals and strategy carried by the people, based on the awareness of the reality and the necessity of letting go of the past. Being united.
II -Meaning	4 **Movement**, People starting to realize what has to be done. Becoming fully aware of their reality. The individual takes responsibility to perform for the better good of the community/organization. Shifting from the 'I' to the 'We'. The people are highly motivated to perform; there is meaning in the thought. 5 **Enlightenment**, objective judgement, distancing, reconciliation. Allowing the community/organization to settle down. Alignment of the mind and Heart (soul). 'We embraces the 'I'. 6 **Liberation**, empowering, liberated from the past, forgiveness. People are inspired by the new concepts / vision. People are manifesting the new vision. Their resistance to transformation and fear for change is dramatically reduced and replaced by a positive feeling of having a purpose and meaning in life.
III -Collective	7 **Community**, purpose, vision carried by the people. People have a strong identity feeling (belonging) and meaning (purpose). The thought /vision becomes reality. 8 **Embracement**, two possibilities: Becoming aware that a higher level of collective consciousness can be achieved. This is where the true Collective (Individual and Collective) reveals itself and the successes of its efforts are consolidated. Start to develop new strategies needed when the not expected happens or for a new level of sustainability. Or If there is an imbalance here – through dogma, arrogance, or complacency in the face of success – then it can undo the entire process. The echo of the ego creates the behaviour of "we are the strongest". The arrogance of the thinking and the knowing. The echo of the ego is a barrier that can create arrogance and dominance. 9 **Full Ending**, the collective embracing their arrogance causing stagnation and ultimately failure or: The collective (organization) moves into a new cycle of prosperity at a higher level of working together.

The ULC is developed as a tool to help nurture better models of leadership and living together, for the individual as well an organization. To have the "I" work better in the context of the "We" in pursuit of outcomes that are beneficial to all, which is called "embracing leadership". What blocks us is our conditioning, the echo of the ego. It hampers our growth to become a fuller person. It limits our full potential.

Embracing leadership

Leaders with angry and resentful egos have traditionally been able to manipulate others through their dominating, convincing language. This leads to destroying other cultures rather than getting to know them.

The echo of the ego inside us blocks us from accessing our inner knowing and taps into the energy of fear and uncertainty, to keep us trapped in the 'command and control' style of duality leadership. When can we recognize that we are being advised by our ego?

The ego adviser:

- Always starts with we saying: 'I don't believe...'
- Management says: 'We need to put better controls in place to protect ourselves against...' and is creating an invisible enemy.
- Fear for survival develops.
- Decisions are taken by an elite group of people, and the collective accepts these decisions, often knowing that the decisions are not right. The invisible energy of resistance and demotivation is a result of not being heard. No opportunity to put the truth on the table and to share the collective knowing.

An informal organization/society develops, with gossiping, complaining and backstabbing, resulting in an unsuccessful working environment with high stress levels, bad communication and demotivated people. History shows us that if the collective stands up to the elite, it is through strikes, revolution, insurrection and war. If we become aware of the embracing leadership philosophy of engaging with the collective and using their wisdom at an earlier phase, we can avoid all these negative power struggles. Employees need to feel that there is a platform for their voices: Lekgotla, a dialogue meeting, an assembly, where every participant has the right to voice his or her view.

The embracing leader always starts creating awareness in the Lekgotla, telling of his/her perception of the problem and consulting the collective for their opinion. Every person has the right to express his or her opinion and, after listening to the different opinions in the collective, the We leader shares with them the final decision he has taken in the Lekgotla. The challenge of a rapidly changing world calls for new patterns of leadership and new behavior, such as We-centered embracing leadership styles. The We leader resonates with the individual's soul wisdom power.

The core leadership values for the new kind of embracing leaders are:

- Trust
- Integrity
- Compassion
- Unconditional love
- Transparency in decision-making
- Sharing wealth
- Belief in people
- Expose them-self's in a collective dialogue to their people

This is the key to us, individually and collectively, becoming part of a natural ecosystem, the reconnection to whom I am and We are.

Organizations are living organisms. They, like humans, have a soul, a collective soul. If we are able to unlock their universal potential, we can create a better world for all. The processes of awareness, reconciliation, forgiveness and letting go of the past are important for creating harmony and unity. The recognition of the collective knowing, an organization's inner truth, is fundamental; it is about the knowing that the mental, spiritual, and emotional energies are in balance. Art can be very instrumental here. The art of the Universal Life Cycle is a guide for working together to become a caring society.

The ULC initiates the proactive process of awareness through which subconscious knowledge, your inner knowing, will be linked to conscious knowing, your thinking. Using the images of the ULC, the cycle creates awareness because it initiates the process of becoming aware, by linking subconscious to conscious knowing. It is the dance/interaction between objective and subjective knowledge and creating/restoring self-consciousness, the alignment of the mind's thinking with the feeling heart, our inner knowing.

Story 3: The Echo of the Ego; the misleading advisor

A dream: The Pondo people of the Transkei. This land, situated in the Eastern Cape of South Africa, is a natural endemic plant and tree hotspot. The Pondo people are a living example of kindness, graciousness and hospitality. They are a testimony to the power of spiritual healing and natural plant therapy. They have indigenous knowledge of how to heal those who have not reconciled with the negative issues in their lives. They respect the land and they live in harmony with an environment of astonishing natural beauty.

The government authorized a license for an international company to start an opencast mine, spanning a significant portion of the area. The rational reason given by government for this decision was that it would create employment. The question is: What happens after the company has extracted all it wants from the soil?

This area could have become a re-energizing center for managers, humans suffering from burnout, to refresh themselves through becoming reconnected with the land and their higher self. In contrast to their short-sighted, false belief decision to create employment, to allow opencast mining in one of the most beautiful and un-spoilt areas on our planet, government could have achieved a better outcome: the creation of long-term sustainable employment in the area without damaging the environment. This could have been achieved by teaching the rational driven world the Pondo people's knowledge of the use of indigenous plants to treat disease, and how they preserved their environment.

If you think about the future, it is clear that this thought could have been Africa's important gift to the world, particularly when we take into account the extremely high usage of medication by Western societies to treat stress-related diseases. Areas like this could be significant in treating stress through natural means, rather than by over-medicating people. It could be the incubator for new economic models. **If it is our sincere wish not to destroy our planet, we need to move from individual wealth to wellbeing.**

Awareness of the We versus the Ego's Echo

Embracing Leaders tirelessly seek to raise awareness about some of the unfortunate legacies of ego. Throughout our history, humanity has sadly struggled with the competition between the "I and the We". The dominance of the ego and the tendency for cultures to dominate one another has brought about one crisis after another throughout humanity's turbulent history.

We can recognize the dominance of the ego in the following labels:

- War on terror
- Global financial crisis
- Jihad
- Developed world
- Undeveloped Third World
- Listen to us, you need to implement democracy
- Need more control mechanisms in place

The dominance of the ego can also be seen in statements showing one person has the wrong perceptions of another whom they do not really know, such as the following statements or behaviors:

- He or she is not reliable
- I deserved that job and not the other person
- Displays of jealousy and anger as well as in the flagrant striving for status

Machiavelli's greatest insight for ego driven organizations was this:

> "For the manner in which men live is so far removed from the way in which men ought to live, that he who leaves the common course for that which he ought to follow will find that it leads him to ruin rather than to safety. For a man who, in all respects, will carry out only his professions of good, will be apt to be ruined among so many that are evil. A prince therefore who desires to maintain himself must learn not always to be good..."
>
> (Source: www.machiavelli.com)

Our challenge now is to create a natural economic system that is sustainable, is gentle to our planet and creates a better quality of life for the collective. Creating this new economic system requires a new evolution of our collective consciousness, one that seeks to serve all. If we are to reverse the damage we are causing to our planet, the only one available to us, we need to build a world that works for all humanity. We need to walk along a different path, one that leaves a natural footprint, where humans are in balance with all the creatures living on this planet and where we nurture and preserve our natural resources. We have been extremely slow in becoming aware of the consequences of our ignorance and the damage we are causing to our planet because it is very difficult to distance ourselves from our individual echo of our ego and false beliefs.

Therefore we need to draw on the richness of culture and cultural diversity. Developing respect for different cultures and an acceptance of cultural diversity is of fundamental importance for the survival of humanity.

It is easier to change behavior than to change culture. Cultural dominance, which creates fear and mistrust, should be avoided at all costs, as it activates our basic instincts for survival, causing us to make decisions that harm the collective. Given the many challenges of the 21st century, it is imperative to draw on the wisdom of cultures that have developed a capacity to work together in mutual trust, peace and harmony. Such cultures, I believe, will have a competitive advantage over others. Every human being should recognize and embrace the fact that culture is the foundation for resilience.

Story 4: Wisdom of the Bratwurst Woman

The heat presses down heavy on the earth. There is no malice in it doing so; it is just the way things are in this land on the southern part of Africa. Along this quiet piece of road is much passing traffic to a local airport. To one side of the hot tar, on a stretch of sand baked hard by the heat and rippled by the fingers of heavy rains, stands an old car, and at the back of it, a trailer made of metal. I stop. Inside, the smell of meat cooking, traditional German sausage dishes, mixes with more African ones. At first glance, the hands that prepare them are those of a simple person. There is some truth in this, but there is also much more depth of complexity.

"It is hot here, Ma."
"I cannot complain. It does not help!"

She greets each new arrival with the energy of a mother. And this is reflected in the way she is addressed by her customers.
"Hello, *Me* (mother)."

"*Sawubona*, Mama." The greeting is the same, no matter the age, culture, or custom of the speaker. It is the recognition of this energy, the role of mother.

"If I don't feel good, the food does not taste good. You cannot cook without love." Here is connection between the mind (as the business woman with customers) and the heart , a human being serving others through putting her positive energy into the food; the result is positive energy, and she is smiling with an open face as she talks to and serves her customers. She is not a slave to the business or customer here, but someone sharing her talents with the world; the quality of her food is testament to this, as it nurtures not only the body but the soul as well, and it contains this energy of love. While we are eating, Molebohe (meaning thank-you) gives us a lecture for free.

"You know, the first words that come out of the mouth are the truth. What comes next is thinking and lies. But why do people like to listen to lies instead of the truth?"

"Think about how much dead energy is traded in the world daily," she said. "Goods that are produced by people who are unsatisfied, demotivated, and certainly not in the mindset of producing with love. This energy is transferred to what is produced. Something empty cannot make another thing full."

I ask her, "Mama, what is your purpose in life, your inner desire"?

"Yes, I know," she answered, with a big smile. "Serving people with love, and that's what I am doing."

For me, this was the not expected: this wisdom and so much positive energy! Thank you, Molebohe.

5 Identity Phase: 1 - Not Expected

We now more fully explore, in this and the following chapters, the three phases of the ULC; Identity, Meaning and Collective.

Identity Phase

1- Not expected	2- Encounter	3- Transformation
Needs a thought	Activate our senses	Manifest awareness
Inside: wisdom	Outside: understanding	Inside: knowledge

Not expected. A surprise, an event, good or bad. To cope with it, you need a thought, an idea/vision not based on thinking, but based on the power of imagination and the wisdom to believe in your inner knowing illuminating the other person. The Not expected requires the infinite thought.

Thought

Thought is received by your soul in a split second, seemingly coming out of nowhere. The soul's spirit transmutes this invisible matter energy into inner knowing, in the mind's subconscious. It translates into an inner desire, vision, imagination or new form of existence.

Tolstoy shared his insight on the topic of thought:

> "*Everything which happens in the lives of human individuals or human societies, has had its beginnings in thought. Therefore, we can find explanations for everything that has happened to other people not in previous events but in thoughts, which occurred before the events took place. In order to change the order of things, either in ourselves or in other people, we must change not events, but the thought, which created the events. Just as one candle lights another and can light thousands of others, so one heart illuminates another heart and can illuminate thousands of others*".

A quote of Martha Graham (dancer and choreographer)

> *"There is a vitality, a life force, an energy, a quickening, that is translated through you into action, and because there is only one of you in all time, this expression is unique. And if you block it, it will never exist through another medium and will be lost".*

Drunvalo Melchizedek writes on the Internet about enlightenment:

> *"In the ancient schools, such as in Egypt, the female or right-brained aspect of the Mystery School (the left eye of Horus) always came first. The students began there working on their emotional healing, and after the emotional healing took place, then the left-brained aspect was taught (the right eye of Horus). Here in the United States, and in other left-brained countries, we have introduced the left-brain studies first, without the emotional healing, because these countries have a difficult time of understanding the female pathway. In many cases, they have simply rejected this simple pathway … Emotional healing is essential if you really wish to find enlightenment in this world".*

With the advance of materialism in the western hemisphere, the emphasis on self-understanding was lost. However, self-examination is making a comeback as society struggles with such emotional afflictions as depression, anxiety, or anger. "Know thyself" was the motto carved in stone on the entrance of the school founded by Greek philosopher Plato. Before any philosophy or discussion, this was the first thought.

Deepak Chopra stated this idea in the following way:

> "Every time you are tempted to react in the same old way, ask if you want to be a prisoner of the past or a pioneer of the future".

The wisdom of the cycle is eternal, a circle that has no start or finish. The "not expected" is the full ending; the beginning is the end, and the end is the beginning. The cycle is an unbroken energy field that is present everywhere in the universe. So inside of the journey to life, the marriage of matter and spirit in our physical body, we find a universal model that can help us understand life in practice. This is the recognition of the inner truth within the self, when the mental, spiritual, and emotional energies are balanced in harmony.

Story 5: The Not Expected a successful surgical separation of two babies.

A professor of neuroscience of the Medunsa University near Pretoria and his American colleague from the John Hopkins University in the United States performed the successful separation of the conjoined twins who were connected at their brains. What was strange for the American specialist was that his South African colleague insisted that a *Sangoma*, a traditional African healer who he trusted implicitly, would be present during the operation. After six hours, the American specialist gave the advice that they should stop the operation, as it would be unsuccessful. The Pretoria professor consulted the Sangoma, who suggested that they take an hour rest before continuing. This process of consultation continued throughout the operation, which lasted twenty-six hours. Later, in 2001, the South African professor gave a lecture at the Erasmus University in Rotterdam about the operation and about the learning. When the audience asked if this experience had brought him success, the answer came as follows: "I am very pleased that God gave me the opportunity to be part of this team to do the operation, but, let me tell you, if this was done in the times of my grandfather, who was a Sangoma, a traditional healer, the collective would have given me one hundred cows. So I am just a blessed professor."

If the professor had followed the false belief of the impossibility of success for the operation by listening to the fear (the echo of the ego) of the other team members, the operation would have been abandoned. Instead he reconnected to the divine essence, the spiritual, with the assistance of the Sangoma; he received the regular instruction to "wait for a while," and see if they were allowed to go on, so he could end the operation with success. The professor listened to his inner knowing and trusted the Sangoma, by-passing the echo of the ego.

The professor was reconnecting intuitively with the essence of life. For all of us it is critical that we again become aware of our existential life journey and that we reconnect with our authentic selves, as it is in that connection that our life pulse originates. While the detail may be complex, the principle is just unconditional love. We need more heart/soul energy in every aspect of daily life. Heart, in its earthbound flow, is the love and affective connection, the essence of emotional intelligence. The heart's energy is the soul of your inner knowing. The miracle of life is that if we find balance and flow, if we are able to embrace our connection with all of life's essence and so manifest polarity, we can all enjoy the unlimited prosperity that is the inextricable result of soul and matter integration. To recognize the universal flow of life and to connect both individually and collectively, in a manner that is in harmonious alignment with your personal being and the collective development potential, is the main purpose of the Universal Life Cycle.

6 Identity Phase: 2 - Encounter: Who am I..?

Encounter. It is an energy flow of understanding in contrast: the response to the not expected; an unexpected gathering or experience to create understanding; dialogue listening to different perceptions. Not frozen in dogma's and false beliefs. It is where individuals are invited to contribute through voicing questions, concerns, and judgment of the new thoughts, voicing their ideas in a positive way.

Awakening: Becoming aware of our false beliefs.

Research suggests that 90 percent of managers take action based on rational analysis of a particular problem or situation. Added to this, only 17 percent of managers invest time in listening to their employees and nurturing relationships. Finally, only 5 percent take time to listen to all of their stakeholders, internal and external. This is a clinical, logic-based, mathematics-type course of action that very often ignores the human component of the overall picture. So why is the reactive approach seemingly so attractive? The temptation may be because it is generally believed that it produces a result quicker and with less work. However, in the long run, such solutions eventually fall down due to a weak foundation based on a fraction of the overall reality, and so they lack sustainability.

Why are many leaders so scared to expose themselves to the public in dialogues? Is their fear missing the natural skills to resonate with the soul energy of their fellow human beings? As a collective and individual we can start executing the principle of awareness, reconciliation and forgiving. Let's rediscover the values of living together in harmony, supporting and thriving for an embracing leadership style on the fundamentals of dialogue and our wisdom within.

The Human Component

Byron Katie in *Loving What Is*, her introduction starts with a quote from Baruch Spinoza:

> "The more clearly you understand yourself and your emotions, the more you become a lover of what is. If you pay attention, you'll notice that you think thoughts like this dozens of times a day. *'People should be kinder' 'I should be more successful.'"* Katie argues these thoughts are ways of wanting reality to be different than it is. This thinking causes all the stress that we feel. We can know that reality is good just as it is, because when we argue with it, we experience tension and frustration. We don't feel natural or balanced. When stopping opposing reality, action becomes simple, fluid, kind, and fearless".

More and more it became clear to me that often we are influenced and conditioned by duality and false beliefs; creating separation.

The awareness that duality does not benefit us as individuals or a collective, and that we need to awaken to the miracle that is polarity and so rediscover unity and balance in ourselves, is of great importance. Thich Nhat Hanh refers to this as "the knots of anger," where he speaks about the search for happiness in the outside world mostly through material sources, as we are told by our culture to do. These internal knots tie us up, cause blockages, and act as limitations on our ability to become what we really are: "a creation of infinite, the universe within."

Story 6: Mr. X in the Pear Tree - an encounter

> His whole life Mr. X had an instinctive feeling for situations that needed a moment of wisdom and thought before rushing in head over heels. Many times, X would hear his inner voice whispering, "Something is not right here—stop, look, listen—be aware!" This led him to the discovery of the phenomenon he calls, the teachings of false belief systems by the knowing and the thinking, those who rule by force as a critical control mechanism of the masses. His world changed when X discovered the level of impact of false belief systems and the extent to which they condition our consciousness and inner knowing. Suddenly X could recognize how people who rule by force use indoctrination of false belief systems as a second nature, to protect their positions and remain in power. It is, in X's view, the most common, most invisible, entrapment of humanity and is manifested in many forms all over the world, disconnecting us more and more from each other and ourselves and feeding the collective pain body of humanity to a level of collapse of the spirit.

As a child, sitting in the top of a very old, huge pear tree, -the world below Mr. X looked so peaceful. The environment around the tree—the birds, the clouds, the sky, and the little city in the countryside—gave him the sensation of being in the Garden of Eden. It was as if God had given him the opportunity to become aware of the beauty of the universe. In the tree, X had many dreams about heaven, what it would look like and how it would feel being there. Many times X walked with his eldest sister in their own Garden of Eden, his sister telling X stories about how beautiful and peaceful it was in heaven. To him, she was an angel, telling him, "You are on earth to search for the truth about life on earth and to teach humanity about harmony and unconditional love." She died in 1946, shortly after the Second World War ended.

If Mr. X had known then...! But X did not pay enough attention to the question of how to live in peace and unity in diversity. Mr. X is now realizing he was captivated by the dogmas and stigmatization of the "thinking and the knowing". Influenced by people in power, the elite telling us what is right or wrong, as well as his own ego. X challenged the world in a court-jester fashion, sometimes being ethically destructive to him self and those X loved. The rebel in him often challenged society in unconventional ways in his quest for answers about the essence and his purpose in life.

Mr. X wanted to understand more about himself and therefore took on a ULC profiling consult. To find out "Who he really was." Mr. X selected images from the ULC needed to create the blueprint for his profile from the nine etches, the source, and the eighteen etchings.

Mr. X's Profile Selections

Before we go discuss Mr X profiles, some observations. One of the most important invisible energies is our Inner knowing (subconscious mind) aligned with our knowing (conscious mind) and the soul's spirit energy. Think about this quote from Hermes: "As above, so below, as within, so without".

The spiral spirit energy of the soul activates the conscious and subconscious mind, explained as an energetic expression in words in the right and left columns below of Mr. X profile.

If we understand the inter action between our conscious and subconscious mind better, the power when these two invisible energies are aligned is unimaginable. The question is - how can we tap into the ocean of infinite wisdom and inspiration; our inner knowing? It is our universe within; we have to discover the wisdom behind the confines of our subconscious mind. What is the person's specific inner knowing fingerprint that resides in his subconscious mind? The confines are our restriction, conditioners, our blockages to become who we really are. When we discover what these confines are, we can become a fuller person. It is our path, roadmap for personal growth.

By doing this the conscious and subconscious mind can form a trinity with the soul's spirit energy, residing in our heart as an invisible partner of matter energy. We may not have expected that we possess a third powerful partner, the soul's spirit energy, the connector between the universe and our universe within.

Inner Knowing: The soul's spiral spirit energy is transmuting infinite energy as an unlimited accessible source for our conscious and subconscious knowing, wisdom, creativity and thought.

This energy also represents our inner 'rainmaker-messenger' in our subconscious mind to manifest the invisible on the screen of the conscious mind as imagination ready for manifestation, to give it form in the physical world. (So inside, so outside)

Mind's knowing Conscious mind energy Etchings 'Without'	Soul transmutes universal energy Thought Soul's spiral spirit energy. 'Within' Etches of the Source	Mind's inner-knowing Subconscious mind energy Etchings 'Without'

Your knowing and inner knowing will simply act upon what resides and vibrates within. This is why visualizations on the screen of our conscious mind, our knowing, the inner TV images from our subconscious mind, our inner knowing, can have such a powerful effect on our personal life's manifestation. If Mr. X is not aware of his inner knowing and soul conditioners, in practice he will find obstructions to access his full potential.

Mr. X - Inner Knowing

He selected the source image, etch plate 2: Encounter:

5) Movement—Mercy	2) Encounter-*Understanding*	11) Movement—*Mercy*
This mind is able to take the visionary ideas and transform them into realistic action. Down-to-earth talent.	This soul's spirit can create understanding. His heart in dialogue with itself creates the energy of balance and alignment and is able to embrace the whole identity. Create form through unconditional love.	This mind can convert thought into meaning that resonates in the hearts of the collective. The feeling is good and reduces fear. This soul is able to unlock the leader in each person.
Left	**Mr. X Selection**	*Potential for growth* **Right**

Mr X Inner knowing

Based on his selection of the source image, etch 2: Encounter – the above represents the full potential of Mr. X if, Mind Logic (left), Spirit Flow (source) and Heart Feeling (right) are in balance.

However in practice, Mr. X was not achieving this potential. His selection from the etchings highlighted the conditioning that was withholding Mr. X from achieving his full potential. Mr. X: Uses **mainly 5** "Movement", from his inner knowing.

Mr. X: Personal Conditioner's Bridge of Inner Knowing

He selected etching 2.

2) Encounter-*Understanding* This mind has an intuitive radar talent for finding the energies that bind the collective.	8) Embracement- *Foundation* The heart (feeling) embracing the ego (thinking mind) as a necessary and enjoyable partner, not as an opponent that must be defeated. Polarity in the physical matter world.	6) Encounter -*Understanding* The mind is able to sense and gain the mental and emotional blockages within the collective or individual. *Potential to become a fuller person.*
Mr. X Conditioner Selection Left	The bridge	Right

Mr. X passing conditioner's the bridge

From his left conditioner selection we see that, for Mr. X to explore his full potential, he has to cross the conditioners bridge passing Embracement and investing more time in the other person's emotions and blockages - the "Encounter" 6. By doing crossing the bridge: Mr.X will develop his potential for growth through tapping in his inner knowing's ocean of wisdom, our subconscious mind.

Mr. X's Profile

Mr. X subconscious mind's inner knowing can create understanding. He is able to convert thought into meaning that resonates in the hearts of the collective. He can inspire and motivate them (feeling). This mind's inner knowing is able to take the visionary ideas and transform them into realistic plans (thinking mind). Most active is his internal radar talent finding the energies that bind the collective. However, due to his subconscious conditioning he is not using his full inner-knowing potential to sense and gain the mental and emotional blockages within the collective or the other person. To activate this, X has to pass the conditioners bridge to embrace the ego as a necessary partner and not as an opponent that must be defeated. To have more understanding for the mental and emotional blockages of the others, Mr. X has to invest more time in the other persons' emotions and feelings. Once again this is Mr. X's potential for personal growth.

It is possible that we are afraid to cross this bridge of our uniqueness due to conditioning. Crossing the bridge can be uncomfortable, but it is the route to go.

Mr. X Talent Selections

Hunter row B2 and row A1
His talents are inspiring the collective with basic ideas or thought. He passes through barriers by catalyzing the commitment of the people.
His pitfalls where talents D12 and emotional F18

Mr. X – The Person

Reading this without knowing the person concerned may make these words somewhat meaningless. So, I will tell you a story about this individual. Mr. X spent many years in the business world. His positions were mostly at a senior management level where he was responsible for restructuring or reenergizing companies. In a strangely natural way, he always seemed to be very good at this, the results coming easily to him. For Mr. X, the people of any company—no matter the size, industry, or location—were the key to drive his plans. By creating unity of purpose within the people, they were the ones that picked up the vision and carried it to execution. His methods were sometimes unorthodox, but then so were the company's achievements; they often went against the trends of the market.

As one can see from his first three selections (soul, dream, inner knowing) much of his ability lies in the collective and identity phase. The words unify, balance, and binding energies appear, suggesting that he has a gift for gaining the commitment of people. If you look further to his talents, you will see this is echoed: inspires and catalyzes commitment. Another ability of Mr. X, one that greatly complimented his ability to unite, was the ability for liberation, shifting boundaries or passing through barriers and creating inspiring thoughts. This was important, as before he could shift a company, he had to focus on reconciliation with the past (be it poor performance or poor company self-image). This was a break from the tendency to blame or scapegoat. Mr. X chose to focus on having the entire collective unite in a proactive, forward-looking way rather than being stuck in a reactive, backward-focused environment. The benefits of the one over the other are obvious, and yet this logic is not always followed; Mr. X was able to achieve this because of his commitment to making a clean break from the past.

Despite his ability to shift people, and therefore companies, there are limitations to Mr. X, just as in everyone. First, Mr. X struggles with words and even more when putting words on paper to express himself. (Emotional F18) It has been a source of frustration, both his and others, throughout his life. Second, Mr. X has a continuous search for balance in the self (spirit and matter). Having limits to his capacity to explain his ideas, he was effective due to his belief in harmony and unconditional love. Mr. X could not easily answer questions about such things as "we organizations." He just felt that the we-oriented organization had a better chance of harmony, prosperity, and sustainability than the "I" or personality based one. The tendency then was to see Mr. X as a curious anomaly, rather than having a unique style or model of leadership. Another side effect of the above limitations was Mr. X's inability to navigate the intense politics of the corporate world. This was particularly so when it came to senior management positions inside of multinational corporations where the environment is often rife with ego-driven and career-obsessed individuals. His answer was always "I don't like politics. I focus on positive energy". He had difficulties to sense the emotional blockages within the collective or individual. To overcome this shortcoming/conditioner he should place emphasis on the feeling heart, embracing the ego as a necessary partner and not an opponent. His purpose in life is to create understanding and awareness.

I am Mr. X; my name is Willem de Liefde.

Something many do not know about me is that I am dyslexic. I grew up in a time before there was the kind of knowledge about, and tolerance of, the condition that we have today. As a result, I was often singled out and blamed for being naughty, for not trying my best, or for cutting corners. The truth is that I could not always translate thought in a way that was easily understood by others. Words and writing have always been difficult for me. Perhaps that is why Jan Montyn came into my life. As an artist, he did not need to read my thoughts in words. Instead he felt them and then created something that does not need words to be explained. The artist Michel van Overbeeke made paintings, and Klaus Elle created images for Mr. X, for it is there where you don't need words to express meaning.

I have always searched for my purpose in life. The ULC made me aware of my inner knowing, my encounter, creating understanding. I feel as if I am starting a whole new journey, because this means, the heart (soul) in dialogue with itself creates the energy of balance and alignment. There is embracement of the whole identity (fuller person) through unconditional love, which creates the form and understanding. The conditioner, the handicap, so to say, was the heart embracing the ego as a necessary partner; that was not always easy in the working/corporate environment.

If I had known then, I could have told my superior to give me another "transformation" job; my specialty is to create understanding, and I can preach that working together in harmony will give excellent results and will give joy in the workplace. But only now do I understand my ego was in the way; I could not embrace it as a good partner. Now I understand, people need time to grow. The result is, I focus more on the other person to sense and gain the mental emotional blockages. Not easy if you have neglected that for so long. I find, having this knowledge, more balance between matter and spirit.

As seen in the story of Mr. X, in the world of duality, Mr. X himself lost a part of who he really was, and he drifted away from his deep inner knowing and desire. Now I feel I am back in the top of the tree. I am grateful for life giving me this opportunity to discover: 'Who am I' and to share with you the wisdom and hidden messages of the ULC, to sustain collective prosperity and meaning.

We as humans have an invisible drive to find our full potential. We know instinctively there is something more inside us. We are not always able to find what it is that drives or demotivate us. The activation of our full, unique finger print: The alignment of our inner knowing (subconscious mind), knowing (conscious mind) and our soul, that is crucial for our wholeness. The original nine etch plates, the source images, are mirroring the soul's energy in matter in your physical body. The selection of one specific etching reflects the active part, the prevailing energy. The conditioned or suppressed potential is our hidden growth potential personal and/ or collective.

Profiling: Who am I-?

Profiling is more full addressed in Chapter 13. However, to assist in gaining familiarity, let us now look at profiling, an imaginary John, just from the last four tables of the full set of nine.

The Nine Profiling Tables:

1	Soul
1a	Soul's conditioner
2	Dream
3	Inner knowing and the conditioners bridge
4	Inner desire
5	Talents and Practical Skills
6	Pitfalls skills and talents
7	Mental and Emotional skills
8	Pitfalls mental / emotional

Note: All Profiling Tables, with comprehensive text explanations, plus the color images selection tables are available in the App and Android tablet version of: "EgosEcho". The App is very user friendly, easily leading the user, step by step, to the creation of his / her profile by selecting an etching image of the original art. An impression of the images in color of the soul and inner knowing are on the front cover and the images of the practical skills at the back cover.

How to select: Intuitively without even thinking, using your gut feeling, your intuition to select one of the nine etches and one of the corresponding etchings.

V-Talents and practical skills

The talents are specific energies that an individual contributes to the collective. From these selections, the individuals will see what they bring to the group setting; this is framed in terms of the rainmaker, hunter, and messenger energies. The talents are the more tangible elements of the individuals' impact on their surroundings. The ULC navigator is a tool for greater self-awareness, assessing the possibilities to better align an individual's talents and abilities.

From the tables below, select two columns, for example column F and column B and select the etching in each column that you feel the most attracted to from your heart—select the one that speaks the most to you.

John's Selections: Row F 15 and Row B 5
F-Acts as guardian of elevated consciousness: The "We" embracing the "I."
B- Makes clear what kind of commitment is needed and what has to be done to realize the vision.
This person has messenger's energy He is able to develop in people very high moral standards, a willingness to take care of each other. Due to his charm and love of people, this person can be a very good translator, speaking to the people about what has to be done.

Note: Given his Messenger energy, probably not the person who inspires a collective. Very good sales order administration manager, executor on a building site, or after sales service where effective communication is paramount.

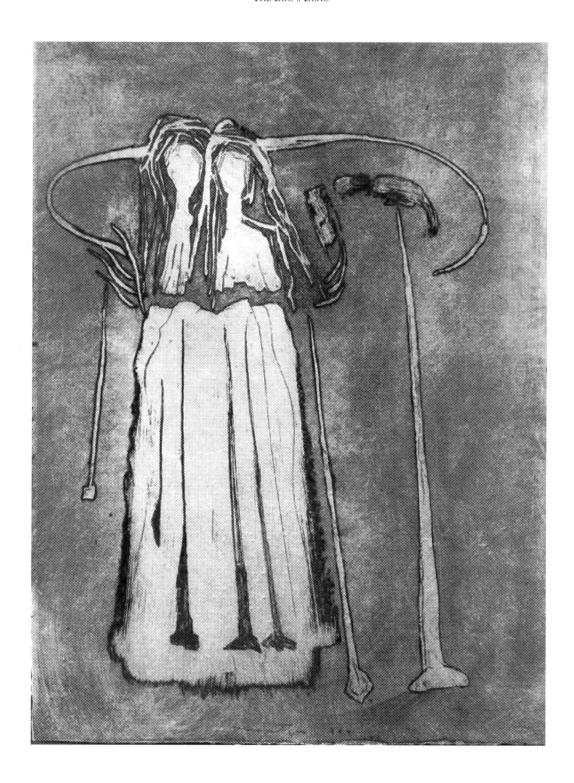

Table V: The Practical Skills/Talents
select two rows and one etching per row

A Rainmaker energy	B Hunter energy	C Messenger energy
1 Inspires the collective with the basic idea or thought.	2 Passes through barriers by catalyzing the commitment of the people to execute the thought/vision.	3 Acts a steward for reconciliation and forgiveness. The custodian of the truth and living in harmony.
4 Shifts perceptions through his natural giving energy of unconditional love for humanity.	5 Makes clear what kind of commitment is needed and what has to be done to realize the vision.	6 Listens through the collective to understand if the vision is still alive or if there are still blockages from the pain of the past.
7 Creates space for change and unity.	8 Reflects on a strategy to see if it is in line with the objectives of the vision.	9 Creates a climate favorable to encourage harmony with the past.
D Messenger energy	**E Hunter energy**	**F Rainmaker energy**
10 Creates liberation from, and a letting go of, the past.	11 Realizing the vision through tangible results. Has the energy of reloading himself with positive energy after a disappointment.	12 Acts as the soul of society and protects the collective from stigmatization through awareness and living in harmony with the past.
13 Reflects on the past to see if the liberation is a reality.	14 By realizing/bringing the results there is the risk of becoming arrogant: I am the best.	15 Acts as guardian of elevated consciousness: The "we" embracing the "I."
16 Creates unity wherein the vision is embraced by the people. Awareness for caring.	17 Achieves more than is expected through being driven by incredibly high standards to perform as collective. Risk of being dominant, overpowering.	18 Always moves through the full cycle, reminding people of the vision and the collective's elevated self.

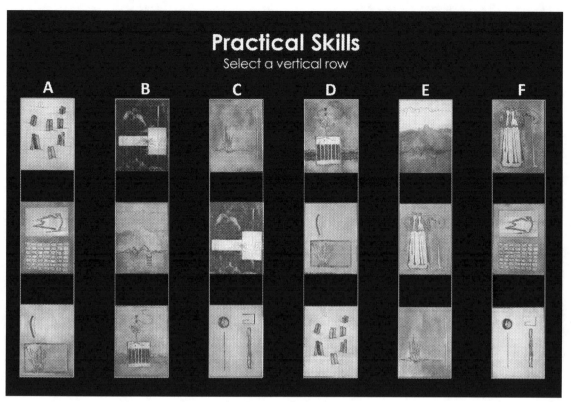

Color image at the back cover

VI - Pitfalls talents/skills

The pitfalls are the obstructions and or conditioners limiting the full energy flow of both our mental, emotional intelligence and the communication with our inner knowing. If individuals are aware of these pitfalls, then they are able to look out for the warning signs bringing unbalanced feelings of unease. The pitfalls are selected from the eighteen etchings.

Table VI - Pitfalls of the talents /skills. Select one of the eighteen etchings you do not like! From the vertical panels		
1 Cannot inspire the collective with the basic idea.	2 Cannot pass through barriers by catalyzing the commitment of the people.	3 Cannot act as a steward for reconciliation and forgiveness.
4 Cannot shift perceptions.	5 Cannot make clear what kind of commitment is needed and what has to be done to realize the vision.	6 Cannot listen through the collective to understand if the vision is still alive or if there are still blockages from the pain of the past.
7 Cannot create space for change and unity.	8 Cannot reflect on a strategy to see if it is in line with the objective of the vision.	9 Cannot create a climate favorable to encourage harmony with the past.
10 Cannot create liberation from and a letting go of the past.	11 Cannot realize the vision through tangible results.	12 Cannot act as the soul of society and protect the collective from stigmatization or assist them in living in harmony with the past.
13 Cannot reflect on the past to see if the liberation is a reality.	14 Cannot realize the vision and give the collective the opportunity or space to move to a higher level of consciousness.	15 Cannot act as guardian of a higher consciousness: The We embracing the I.
16 Cannot create unity where the people embrace the vision.	17 Cannot achieve either; a higher level of collective consciousness creating space for sustainability and innovation	18 Cannot move through the full cycle, reminding people of the vision and the Collective's higher self.

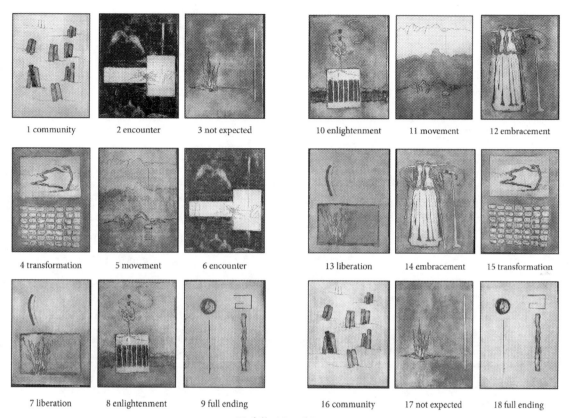

Pitfalls 18 etchings

The Pitfalls of the Skills/Talents

John's selection; one of the eighteen etchings from vertical panels John **did not like.**
Selection 4, which speaks for itself: Cannot shift perceptions

VII - Mental and Emotional skills

The mental skills and emotional intelligence (soft stuff) are those individual abilities that, again, have an impact in the collective setting. They are thinking and feeling abilities, both tangible and intangible, that individuals bring to bear in the group.

Table VII The Mental/Emotional skills Select two horizontal rows Select one image per selected row.		
A	1 Emotion	2 Senses	3 Intuition
B	4 Deep thinking	5 Spirituality	6 Great wisdom to avoid arrogance
C	7 Boundary shifting	8 Liberation	9 Boundary drawing
D	10 Harmony from the heart	11 Responsibility	12 Ethical and moral choices
E	13 Stability	14 Reliability—being the cornerstone of society	15 A disciplined moderator
F	16 Creativity of mind and soul	17 Energy of innocence	18 Talent for speech and/or writing

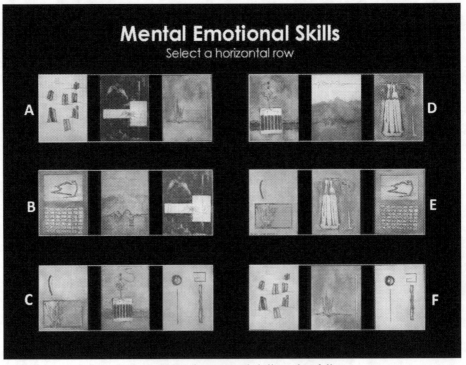

Images mental emotional skills and pitfalls

John selected: C7 Boundary shifting and A3 Intuition
John can rely on his softer skills, such as intuition, for the moving of boundaries.

VIII - The Mental/Emotional Pitfalls

The pitfalls are the obstructions that can, and do, limit the full energy flow of both the talents and mental and emotional skills.

Table VIII - The Mental/Emotional Pitfalls			
Annexure: Image table III select **one** of the 18 etchings you **don't** like! From the horizontal panels			
A	1 Shows no emotion	2 Senses	3 Has no intuition
B	4 Unable to think deeply	5 Not spiritual	6 Not wise and cannot avoid arrogance
C	7 Unable to shift boundaries	8 Not liberated	9 Unable to set boundaries
D	10 No harmony from the heart	11 Does not take responsibility	12 Does not make ethical and moral choices
E	13 Not stable	14 Weak Reliability—not a cornerstone of society	15 Not a disciplined moderator
F	16 Not creative in mind	17 Not flexible/suspicious	18 No talent for words and/or writing

John's Selection F 17: Not flexible/suspicious from the 18 etchings
The pitfalls of Mr. John can be a contra indication when flexibility is needed.

This brief example gives an indication of how quickly a useful profiling can be obtained from a manager or management team, developing a higher state of awareness to form a strong united team.

The Impact on Leadership

Knowing: Who am I and letting go of the past are the gateways to a new kind of leadership, and for cultures working in harmony with each other.

Awareness is fundamental here and is linked to logic, reason and perception but comes from a deeper place in our being. It is linked more closely to the heart and the soul and forms a key ingredient in the transformative impulse. Respecting each culture is the foundation of accepting one another, a foundation that must be flexible and strong. There is trust and freedom of speech, listening to the other person with an open mind. The people and organization/society are awareness-oriented.

An embracing leader's vision resonates with the people's soul. He creates an energy spiral of new thoughts and passion for the possibilities of people's future. This energy activates awareness in the soul and mind of collectives having a purpose. It is Proactive rather than Reactive leadership.

The Reactive approach versus a Proactive approach

Story 7: Reactive approach—Cyprus in 2013

The recent freezing of Cypriot bank accounts, together with the suggestion that depositors would be debited in order to pay for the country's bailout, sent shock waves around the world. The reason for this perhaps, was the fact that it happened literally overnight and without warning. The story read like a tale of thieves in the night. Surprise, dismay and then anger followed. Rather than engaging those potentially affected in dialogue (identity) toward agreeing on a path of action (meaning), so as to have each link in the chain accept the proposal and be a willing part of it (collective), the "powers" imposed their will. Because of the lack of communication and shared decision making, the people lost trust in the leadership of the "thinking and the knowing."

This duality approach always results in: Demotivation, being depressed, egocentric behavior.

Story 8: Proactive approach - "We Have a Problem!"

An embracing leader preparing an encounter for transformation

"We have a problem" is a statement concerning a truth that is universally understood. However, in reality the perception of what is the root or cause, the solution even, will have a lot more to do with the coach, manager or individual's truth. For example, in a team sport an individual may feel that a lack of competent coaching staff has limited her ability to give her team the kind of specialized attention it needed. On the other hand, some team members may feel that the captain or the lack of a competent point scorer is a problem, while others may feel the coach/manager/leader alone is to blame, never the individual. Potentially there are as many perceptions as to the cause of the problem as there are members of the team, each one having his or her own perception of the truth. Mainly, the problem is always looked at as outside of us.

In reality, the problem is everywhere it is perceived to be. The general response to such situations is to call a meeting where the problem is expressed and discussed by a select group of people who represent the entire collective. Let us call them *the thinking and the knowing*. This group, through a discussion, formulates and decides on a solution, which is then presented to the group as the solution. Alternatively, the collective goes into the dialogue of disconnect. This is characterized by posturing, argument, and disagreement as different individuals or camps form within the collective (silos), each one pushing its own agenda and positioning itself to be the one to create, drive, and take credit for the solution. Because it seems that there is so much at stake, there is generally fear of the truth, maybe even a desire to manipulate or conceal it. The result is frustration, unhappiness, and division within the collective—the opposite of what is needed in times of crisis—and so the solution tends not to stick or is unsustainable. Now imagine the same scenario handled in a different way by a leader knowing who they can be one.

Story 9: Continued

The coach calls the entire collective together—players, both junior and senior; club owners; coaching and support staff; administration officials; cheerleaders; and representatives of the fan club—basically everyone who is associated with the team. Standing before the assembled collective, the coach, head held high, speaks her heart: "We have a problem! We all know it, but I do not know exactly what it is or how to begin fixing it." The coach's words reverberate through the room like the ripples of a bomb blast. Each individual recognizes honesty for what it is and feels its truth. As a collective, individuals look to themselves and to one another. There is recognition that this is their truth. Yes, there is an element of shock that someone could be so honest, be so vulnerable, but the gesture is a welcome relief. In this environment, such a gesture could even be used against her and yet the coach does not falter. She continues: "I need your help! Together we can find a solution." There is a further stirring in the collective. Something invisible begins to build in the room. She says, "Each one of us needs to look into ourselves to find an answer. Then we can put our heads together, come to agreement, and create a plan as to how we move forward." The dialogue has begun and each voice has been invited to be a part of the conversation, to give advice and to guide a solution. Whatever the outcome each individual and the collective will be affected.

Imagine this scene for a second, the kind of thoughts and emotions that would go with it, the impact. Does such an approach not have the greatest potential for prosperity? Through the recognition that a chain is as strong as its weakest link rather than weak because of it, that all parts are necessary to create and sustain an optimal whole, the coach has started something. Given the chance, each part becomes aware of the importance of its role and its contribution to the whole. Inspired, each link strives to perform to the best of its ability—the individual in the collective, the collective in the individual. The approach of the imaginary coach is an interesting one. It is an example of the proactive approach. While we may not be able to think of actual examples of such an approach, the potential of such a strategy surely resonates. Every CEO, leader, captain, and individual can introduce this style of embracing leadership, sharing the truth; its energy is an unconditional giving energy, letting go of the past and reducing fear, and above all, listening to all the voices without prejudice.

Awareness is fundamental here and is linked to logic, reason and perception but comes from a deeper place in our being. It is linked more closely to the heart and the soul and forms a key ingredient in the transformative impulse that accompanies the process of letting go, which is essentially for acceptance. Culture is the foundation of accepting one another, a foundation that must be flexible and strong. There is trust and freedom of speech, listening to the other person with an open mind. The organization/society is awareness-oriented.

This polarity approach, listening to all the voices, accessing the collective wisdom creates purpose around the common goal.

7 Identity Phase: 3 - Transformation

Transformation: Through awakening to and embracing acceptance of the vision by the people, there is agreement around its truth. This builds a climate of trust so that balance and harmony are possible inside of change—alignment and common purpose. They vibrate in the individual and collective, shifting perceptions and beliefs. The transformation brings a higher state of awareness of the identity. If we, as organizations and societies, can work together in the paradigm of unconditional love heart energy, the crewmembers of the organization will feel positively guided in feedback. This uplift generates a pulse of positive energy, vibrating through the collective (crew) giving them the joy to perform for the good of the whole organization or society.

The Voice of the People

One of the traps we find ourselves in is our addiction to our thought patterns, dogma's and rational thinking. As a result, we tend to move directly into action, without sufficiently exploring the deeper consequences of doing so from a feeling good or bad perspective. We forget to listen to our inner knowing.

Companies with unhappy employees are losing billions of dollars a year because their employees are disengaged from their workplace, resulting in poor productivity. Cape Town psychologist Jeanne Lu Bruwer says: *"Employee disengagement is a worldwide problem, with Gallup research showing that the US economy lost between $287 billion and $370 billion a year as a result of disengagement".*

She also wrote: *'Employees need to feel that there is a platform for their voices. When people are told how to do their work, they cannot be more creative and innovative as they are restricted to conform'.*

Think about engaging and embracing leadership listening to the wisdom of the people. How many Collectives find them selves in this kind of situation? The result can be a lack of motivation and common purpose around the goal. Individuals work against one another in silos when their wellbeing fundamentally depends on cooperation to create a new vision (thought). It is crucial that we keep a constant awareness as to the importance of identity, meaning, and collective being balanced. They are key elements in human social endeavors. It may appear that consideration of these phases is only necessary in times of difficulty, but it should apply even more in times of prosperity. The transformation phase then becomes a metaphor for harmony, prosperity, and sustainability. If we look to a human body where one of the necessary organs is not functioning, we see that eventually that failing organ will begin to affect those dependent on it and finally affect the whole. If the ailment is not properly diagnosed, even if the recommended medication should gain some ground in treating the symptom, it may not result in a cure because of being focused on a wrong, though connected, cause or source.

The conscious mind thinking is where we get stuck because it keeps us a prisoner of the physical world and a prisoner of the logic of duality—it stops us from reconnecting our subconscious mind with the soul's spiral spirit energy and the super consciousness, the ocean of knowing the univers from which we all came.

The Truth Is

Universe's super consciousness knowing is imprinted in each and every matter-based physical body cell, as inner knowing memory. This is the energy that the spirit [unconditional love], mind [knowing] and soul [inner knowing] bring with them as they come into the physical body. They come from unity and manifest as polarity at the moment of birth. When spirit comes into matter and the physical process begins, matter consciousness results in us as conscious and subconscious mind and soul's spirit.

Matter consciousness is purely physical matter oriented. Its focus is on life in the physical world. The ego, or our thinking self (the mind), is an energy that is concerned with action or tangible results and so, logically, is that part of us that most often becomes dominant. At the same time, emotion, our feeling self (heart), is also an energy that is imagination, wisdom and form oriented. Through our conditioning, our emotions are purely concerned with, or in relation to, something else in the physical world. We tend to oscillate between the three sides of the self: the "I" of the mind, the "We" of the heart and our inner knowing.

Because our experience is physical, through the senses, we come to take this as the ultimate reality. Through the experience of the material world we lose touch with the metaphysical (thought energy), our inner knowing (subconscious mind). We become fixated on the physical and come to the belief that this is all there is. If it cannot be seen, heard, smelt, felt, or tasted, it cannot be. In truth though, this represents only a marginal part of our complete being, but a very dominant one manifested by the ego and false belief ideology.

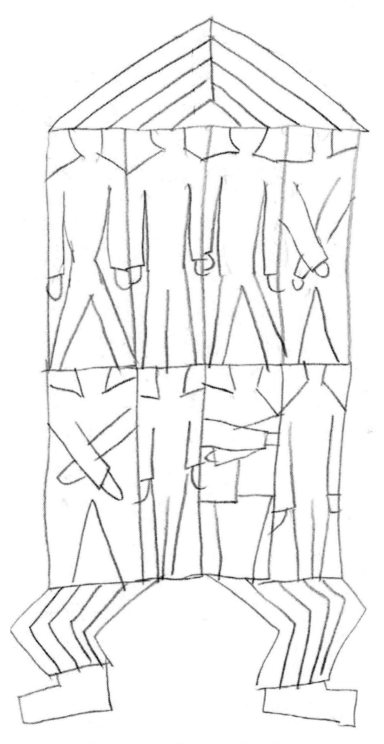

Prison of the conditioning-by Klaus Elle

Search for Balance

Balance is key for any individual or collective to be whole. The ideology of duality has caused significant damage to the individual, collective, and even the earth. Things that are meant to be one through the act of balance are ripped apart, something that goes against the natural order of polarity. As mentioned before, polarity is the logic that orders the world of matter and spirit. It has, for many people, the illusion of being similar to duality. Polarity is the energy flow between the mind (logic) and the heart (feeling), not as opponents but as partners in diversity. Like the magnetic energy flow between the north and south poles—a positive energy needed for navigation on earth that is used by sailors, birds and fish.

Vusamazulu Credo Mutwa is a Zulu high Sanusi, the highest level initiation healer, thought to be the last in South Africa and one of only two remaining on the African continent. He is a custodian of umlando (tribal history) and culture. Mutwa said, "[We] live in a strange world of separatism: a world in which things that really belong together, and which ought to be seen as a greater whole, are cruelly separated."

The trouble with life is finding a way to peel off the layers of conditioning and fear we have accumulated. This is only possible if you know whom you are (an internal force) and if you are not governed by the dogmas of false belief (an external force). The false beliefs we accept from the external world can have a hold on our internal world.

The life cycle can be of help here.

When an individual is able to put words to an understanding of the self, there is a kind of road map from which to look at the self as well as the self in the world. When we have words or concepts through which we can make sense of our strengths and talents, or our stumbling blocks, we have beacons by which we can navigate our way in the world.

Story 9: Signs of Hope for a natural economy and living in harmony with all there is.

If all our leaders were able to tap into their inner knowing, they could access the collective wisdom that has existed in societies for millennia. Through this collective consciousness, they could create a new, gentle kind of natural economy for humanity. In the following passage, Unilever chief Paul Polman talks to Jo Confino about the company's radical sustainability agenda.

> Who would have thought, even a few years ago, that one of the world's most powerful chief executives would be advocating a transformation in society

far more radical than any mainstream politician. Paul Polman, the CEO of Anglo-Dutch consumer giant Unilever, says the political and economic systems are failing and that capitalism needs to be reframed to work for the common good. Too many companies have prospered at the expense of society and nature, and that business now has to learn to be successful while contributing to society and supporting ecosystems and biodiversity. "We do not have to win at the expense of others to be successful," he says. "Winning alone is not enough; it's about winning with purpose." He acknowledges the Occupy Wall Street movement for exposing the inequalities in society, warning that this is just the tip of the iceberg and that companies that fail to respond to the social and environmental challenges of our age are at risk of being put out of business. "The Occupy Wall Street movement sends out a very clear signal," says Polman. "If you look out five or ten years, which is my job, the power is in the hands of the consumers, and they will not give us a sense of legitimacy if they believe the system is unfair or unjust. Some companies that miss the standards of acceptable behavior to consumers will be selected out. I am not advocating communism or trying to turn the world into a *kibbutz*. Some people sometimes accuse me of being a socialist, but I am a capitalist at heart. What I want is a sustainable and equitable capitalism. Why can't we have that as a model?"

Paul Polman, is acknowledged as one of the leaders of a small but growing band of progressive companies that believe humanity is heading for disaster unless politicians, companies, and civil society join forces to respond to the challenges of social injustice, climate change, resource scarcity, ecosystem degradation, and biodiversity loss. "We have increasing income disparity within the developed world. We have a political system that barely functions after the economic and financial crisis. So continuing the way we are going is simply not a solution. Increasingly, consumers are asking for a different way of doing business and building society for the long term together."

Awaken the Universe Within

Within each of us is the latent capacity to achieve, to be our full selves. We have talents and energy that need to find expression in our everyday lives, bringing reward to ourselves and our community. When the Individual role is aligned to the vision of the community, the community in turn gives support to the Individual, giving a healthy Collective. Achieving this utopia of personal expression, in harmony with the vision of the community, requires Embracing Thought Leadership and Individuals who are free of their conditioning, who have been able to let go of the past and trust in their true selves.

The thought leads to the awareness of letting go of the past, an enormously powerful energy for sustainability, reducing fear and creating new forms of balanced economies and societies, an ongoing alignment process of heart and mind.

Studies by well-known universities suggest that 80 percent of restructuring and mergers within companies fail. Why? This is because leaders in such situations are not aware of the need to guide their people through the process of awareness and dialogue. But how many leaders are prepared to talk about such things? This is the so-called soft stuff. And yet, for many organizations, this is the Achilles' heel.

The Trinity Represents the Totality

What the ULC brings is methodology through a Trinity matrix structure and the use of art to guide people through awareness, dialogue and forgiveness on the road to achieving a life of fulfillment and harmony.

In the table that follows, the center column represents the original nine images, the source, while left are the thinking mind and right, the feeling heart energy .We need to come back into the flow of polarity if we are going to unlock the power of trinity, specifically for working together in harmony in a multi-cultural society.

Left	Center	Right:
"I think, therefore I am."	"I am that I am."	"I am because we are."
I	Unity (infinity)	We
Thinking /logic/analytical Mind	Soul's spiral spirit energy	Feeling /Emotion
Manifest	Thought	Subconscious mind
Conscious mind	Unconditional love	Thought to be understood

Each of these three energies has abilities, but there are also limitations in terms of what they can achieve. This is where balance, through the interaction between them, becomes so important. The Trinity works because there is interdependence. Think about this Trinity in relation to the Trinity we introduced at the beginning of the book: Identity, Meaning and Collective.

Alone, or individually, every individual has gifts and talents that only become truly meaningful when they are working in the service of others (Collective). They bring balance to the different parts by enhancing (or heightening) individual talents. Importantly, the Collective also gives support to individual shortcomings or weaknesses of the individual.

The ULC trinity matrix extends our understanding further, building a detailed picture of the complex reality. The trinity matrix can give a deeper level of analysis of what is needed at what stage, as a Collective moves through the cycle. For now, let us focus on explaining the trinity matrix in principle. The ULC is a roadmap for change and sustainable transformations.

The most fundamental question: How to implement this in daily life?

The ULC's process of letting go of the past is an ongoing process of awareness, taking into account the forces of resistance and perceptions of the individuals.

How do we achieve a healthy Collective? This happens when the Individual, shares their unique talents and abilities and so unlocks the wisdom of the collective, agreeing a shared vision. Each Individual contributes in a role best suited to their strengths, with the Collective in turn providing the Individual with support in this role. And so this relationship reciprocates, self-sustains, two poles feeding and being fed by one another. This is Polarity the power that orders the world of matter.

It is pure partnership; alignment of the conscious – and subconscious mind with the soul, heart's spirit energy and a continuous energy stream through communication, between the three separate but fundamentally interdependent connected entities due to continues communication. This is best represented by the symbol for infinity:

So, fundamentally, and by definition, the Collective needs the Individual, and the Individual the Collective. The one's existence is premised on the existence of the other.

The Individual needs: Identity, Meaning and Collective to unlock its potential inside of a Collective. The Collective needs: Thought, Senses and Awareness, to unlock the potential of each Individual within the group.

These entities, dependent and interrelated energies are in the lifecycle matrix also: Thought, Feeling and Manifest. ULC's navigator is a detailed guideline, guiding the individual in the process of the echo of one's true self, transcending the ego's echo, to become a fuller person and collective. The logic that works simply through the artwork, the etchings in different colors, the etched plates, evades description in words.

The three energies are a trinity

"All these primary impulses, not easily describable in words, are the springs of man's actions."
                                                Albert Einstein

First intersection of the Identity phase; - Not Expected.

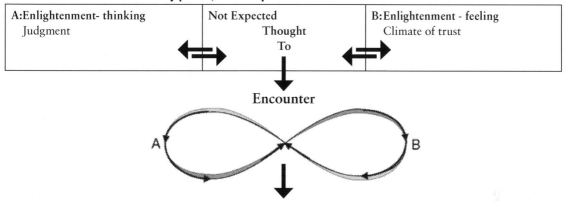

A:Enlightenment- thinking Judgment	Not Expected Thought To	B:Enlightenment - feeling Climate of trust

Encounter

Than to the next intersection: - **Transformation**
And so on.

Identity, Meaning, and Collective are informed by the external but can only become meaningful when accepted internally. Awareness, Reconciliation, and Forgiveness, on the other hand, are products of the internal world, but become meaningful when expressed externally.

Using the ULC-navigator, we create an awareness of this dance of infinity, continuously understanding the dynamics between the diverse individuals and the collective in the intersections of the ULC. If the **Not Expected** happens, you have to encounter the **Enlightenment** from the thinking side **A,** as well as the **Enlightenment** from the feeling side **B.** Then embracing leadership can bring these first intersection in balance.

You can navigate to the next intersection, **Encounter**, and again here we take the **Movement** from the thinking side **A** and the **Movement** from the feeling side B and when in balance, go to the **Transformation**, and so on through all the phases. The three phases fuse as one flow. To explain the process better, stories are added between the phases Identity, Meaning and Collective.

Phase I: Identity roadmap for transformation and change.

Step 1

Enlightenment—*Judgment* Take a helicopter view. Objective logic judgment of the thought and the unexpected event. A	1) Not expected—*Wisdom* A not expected event, fear for the future. Rainmaker energy is called to action for a thought/ idea. Envisioning.	Enlightenment—*Judgment* Question: Does the thought or idea resonate in the people's heart? Setting a climate of trust. Mirroring people's feelings of the reality. B

Step 2

Movement—*Mercy* Down-to-earth solutions. Awareness of "Why are we here in this situation today?" A	2) Encounter— *Understanding* Open dialogue, every voice is heard. Listen to people's fear and ideas and their view on the vision/thought /ideas through raising questions. The hunter makes it practical, understandable, and judgmental for the people.	Movement—*Mercy* There can be no movement without an emotional and mentally based awareness and understanding of the perceptions, thought and feelings in the people's hearts. B

Step 3

Embracement- *Foundation* WE together align the people. Where perceptions are shifting, so they are prepared for the altering course. A	3) Transformation – *Knowledge* Formulating the new goals and strategy based the reality and a new vision/ideas and the necessity of letting go of the past. New goals and strategies are communicated. The identity gets its form. Passing first barrier ∞	Embracement—*Foundation* Are the perceptions, feelings and beliefs actually shifting? The emotional part is the acceptance of the "We" at the level of self. The messenger's role is very important in the creation of confidence in the "I" and the "we." B

Story 10: The fire-resistant door, reenergizing identity at the workplace

A 'We' organization develops a lightweight door that is fire resistant for more than an hour, while the doors produced by their competitors are fire resistant for only half an hour. This 'We' organization is a newcomer to the market and decides to launch its product at the country's Fire Brigade and Fire Protection Products Fair, for the building industry, fire brigades and regulators of the government. The company selects a stand next to the exhibition of the fire brigade' cars stand. The 'we' organization has high expectations that many patrons at the fair will visit its exhibition, but is disappointed when, on the first day, its exhibition attracts interest from only a handful of firefighters and no visits from property developers, architects or anyone in the building or real estate industries.

The director of the 'We' organization arranges a dialogue with his staff that very afternoon, taking full responsibility for the mistake, which comes as a big relief for the employees, who had been sure they would have to take the blame (false belief echo). During the dialogue, they come up with a number of solutions, none of which, unfortunately, proves to be realistic. The director has just announced his decision to reduce the number of staff at the fair when the commander of a major city fire department, who entered their exhibition space during the meeting and joined their discussion, spoke up.

The Not Expected happened:

The fire brigade commander's Thought: 'Place a full-page advertisement in the major national papers with the simple words:

> "Half an hour of fire resistance is not sufficient. We believe the minimum requirement is one hour".

The Encounter

The atmosphere of employees at the Encounter changed from pessimistic, we are stupid and so on to 'Yes we can'. No more the feeling being the victim of the Echo of the Ego. The staff members at the fair became excited about this thought.

The Transformation

The director decides to go ahead and to place the advertisement. They manage to get the advert published that very day. The following morning, their stand is crowded with people from the building industry, fire departments and government regulators. Soon after this, the government became their biggest supporter. In addition, many other potential end-users embrace their product. Very soon this product became a great success in the market.

This action unites the hearts of all the people involved. It is a good example of how the embracing leadership, laying the foundation of the identity, starts creating a strong sense of meaning, internally as well by the external environment of this company.

Summary remark - Identity phase ULC:

IDENTITY *is a strong visionary energy that binds individuals together and limits fear. It is the first, fundamental, step to sustainability, cooperation, and unity of purpose. This phase creates a sense of purpose and paves the way for transformation towards meaning.*

Story 11: Wisdom Within

An example of a positive use of technology and a thought/vision can be found in the instance where a multinational supermarket chain started an organic food division. It recognized that small-scale farming led to living in harmony with the environment. To this end it began to work in Malawi. The supermarket company made use of local packaging, people's knowledge of sharing and dialogue with the community for problem solving. It came up with techniques that did not rob the land of its vital nutrients. In addition, importantly, the old ways of farming gave the community a sense of meaning. Small-scale farming in Malawi has since had great success.

In a similar vein, there is much land lying fallow. If some of this underutilized land was given to the local people to farm, food could be produced for subsistence and commercial uses. This would also give people back their dignity and would stop the areas from becoming ghettos of poverty. Through this collective consciousness they could create a new, gentle kind of natural economy.

Identity Phase:

Not expected - Thought	Encounter- Senses	Transformation- Awareness
Wisdom	Understanding	Knowledge
Archbishop Buti Tlhagale said to the president of South Africa, Jacob Zuma, "I hope that your first priority will be nation-building, healing and continuing to heal our much scarred souls."	Khalil Gibran wrote, "When we turn to one another for counsel, we reduce the number of our enemies."	Lao Tzu said, "If you want to awaken all of humanity, then awaken all of yourself; if you want to eliminate the suffering in the world, then eliminate all that is dark and negative in yourself. Truly, the greatest gift you have to give is that of your own self-transformation."

8 Meaning Phase: 4 - Movement

Meaning phases

4-Movement	5-Enlightenment	6-Liberation
Feeling passion/trust	Give insight awareness	Frees from false beliefs/fear
	Balance through reconciliation	Through forgiveness
Outside: Mercy	Inside: Judgment	Outside: Beauty

Movement. Movement converts the thought or vision into feeling resonating in people's heart. It is the truth in words that radiates and inspires through touching strong emotions, the beginning of the vision as meaning. It is the feeling that this is right, unlocking energy for starting the process to manifest. It is connecting the scientific, analytical with the spiritual.

Movement: The quality of communication that's binding, giving people a good feeling based on understanding and knowledge. When there is trust people want to share their knowledge. It is an event to be grateful for, mercy.

Story 12: Chaos in the Mass Mind

In their daily lives people frequently perceive life as 'being disconnected, chaotic and threatening'.

> The queues have grown slowly as more and more people filter in. At first there is an order to this. The crowd's movement is an ebb and flow, calm and with a universal logic. The mood of people is upbeat, friendly and excited. The young and old mix together freely; different cultures and backgrounds are together. But as the minutes become hours, as the seconds fall off the clock, things start to change. The earlier ease begins to show signs of building tension. Each individual wants to be among the first to enter through the doors of the mall on the first day of the massive clearance sales, to beat the rest to the queue for registration, to stand out in the grand procession or parade. An invisible trigger sparks something in the group. One person breaks ranks, pushes, and runs.

Before their minds can take stock and assess the situation, others follow. Basic instinct/mass mind, like a wildfire, catches hold and madness flows; people trample one another under indiscriminate foot; children and the elderly are shoved aside. Grabbing, pushing, pulling, punching ensue. "I must be first!"

Soon calm returns, for such frenzied energy cannot be maintained for long. Confusion sets in. People ask themselves, "What happened?" All around, broken bodies lie amid the pieces of what was once the source of collective desire. People ask themselves, "How did this happen?" What was meant to be so simple, so ordinary, took on the qualities of chaos and anarchy. There was enough to go around. Everyone was able to share in what was there. But how could there be sharing when all individual and collective senses of right momentarily disappeared? Eventually, as reason returned, people were faced with themselves. The mass-mind subsided and the individual became aware of himself or herself once again. The smell of wild contagion hung on each being. The gentle and peace-loving individuals stood, stunned, horrified by the blood on their hands. They asked themselves that most difficult question, not really wanting to hear the answer. Was that really me?

The question arising: How to avoid this hunter-warrior behavior?

When the heart is the energy that drives us in the physical world, there is no need for fear. Trust is the guiding light. The key question is how do you open up the talents of the "I" in the domain of the "We"? The general reaction is for us to ask, "What do I need to do?" Our focus often turns straight to action, typically ignoring the process of fully engaging with the source or cause of the problem. The disappointment comes when we do not succeed, and the reaction is to focus on disappointment, blame and anger. "I should have …" "I wish I …" "That product was bad." All of these responses look to the past and pass blame on the outside world—"The problem was not me"—and yet the situation remains. If our thoughts (or identity) and feelings (or meaning) are aligned then whatever it is we desire will manifest (or collective). More than five thousand years of duality have left its mark on us. I can imagine you will think more than five thousand years, yes more than and so, as individuals and collectives, there is much work to do. These conditioners will not just vanish the moment we decide we want them to.

Martin Luther King; "*Men often hate each other because they fear each other; they fear each other because they don't know each other; they don't know each other because they cannot communicate; they cannot communicate; because they are separate*".

Conversation with Quinton Coetzee

When struggling with the understanding of the impact of matter on the human mind—specifically what role it plays or how it interacts and influences that thinking mind, a thought came. I phoned Quinton Coetzee, a natural scientist, conservationist, and presenter of wildlife television programs. Immediately, he went into story mode. The insights carried on his words nicely illuminated this field of inquiry, giving me the perspective of someone who looks at the world with a scientific eye. Matter was created by source. Some may look at this event as creation, while others may refer to it as the big bang, source being the causal energy that gave life to these processes. These two are by no means reflective of the countless understandings and interpretations by the peoples and cultures of the world. The point of commonality across this range or systems of beliefs is that they all have a beginning—something came into being that was not previously there.

"Our biggest question in science today is "How did life start?" came the voice on the other side of the phone.

"What is agreed on is that the material world as we know it is about 4.5 billion years old. From the moment of its beginning, various organisms and creatures have grown and evolved over millions of millennia until the present, with human life being but a split second in this span of history. "It is estimated that nearly 100 percent, let's say 99 percent, of everything that ever existed on this planet is now extinct through the six major extinctions as well as other factors. So, 1 percent of what lives here today—us included—has withstood ice, fire, meteor bombardment, possible magnetic shifts in the planet, tides, earthquakes, and so on."

That was quite a statement, but what he said next just deepened the feeling about source and our belief that everything in matter originates from unity. "Everything comes from one biological source in an unbroken chain. We, as the 1 percent that is left, are the representatives of what has survived in this chain that goes back 4.5 billion years."

All this made sense, but what about the notion of thought, about its coming from source with an individual's unique fingerprint or purpose? Did it have a place in this matter-based story? Posing the question to Quinton, his response only increased the wonder. "All life forms are completely unique in their makeup. Do you know that the Australian koala has unique fingerprints, just like humans?" Imagine seal pups on the beach, their numbers in the thousands. How do mothers, returning from feeding in the ocean, find their pups in this sea of life? This speaks to the uniqueness of all living things. Each tree of the same species looks the same, but one would be hard pressed to find two that were identical in shape and size.

Interestingly, Quinton told this story from Barberton in South Africa's Mpumalanga Province. The mountains and exposed rock that surround this former mining town are some of the oldest in the world, dating back around 3.5 billion years. The rocks appear pale grey-green and are dramatically accentuated by the sharp rise and fall of slopes and peaks and the dance of sunlight and shadow. These ancient structures have given up many secrets of the surface conditions on very early Earth, including what is thought to be the first form of life on planet, a bacterial micro fossil, *Archaeospheroides barbertonis*.

Quinton commented that we human beings have as much difficulty in our attempt to describe the physical world of matter in the absolute as we do when it comes to the nonmaterial or spiritual world. Our attempts at knowledge or explanation seem to have taken humankind on a journey toward disconnecting from the very things we are so desperate to capture and describe. Quinton said, "Did you know that, apart from a human being, there is only one other organism on earth that consumes everything in its environment before moving on? The virus!" These nonchalant words pounded the senses and shook understanding. Could it be true that we, like the virus, have the logic of self-destruction, the human virus? We are looking through the shell we are outside of, and we are trying to push on it to make a hole through which we can look back in. So, is the human, is humanity, doomed to a fate written by its own hand? Are we meant to join the 99 percent that are now extinct?

No! It would seem that this is the fate of modern man, but there are still remnants of a human past where there was no history or time, just life and a people who lived it. Ironically, they were pioneers of sustainability, whose way of life has been decimated through contact with modernity, the very same destructive modernity that is now so obsessed with becoming sustainable.

Quinton was born in the Namib Desert and grew up in one of the lands of the Khoi San people. Stone Age "primitives," the Khoisan (bushmen), the San people—all look at the world from the inside out (the natural way.) We look from the outside in. Quinton continued with a question, "When was this turn? When did we shift to this other way?"

My answer was: "For me Quinton, that was at the time of the tower of Babel and the first warrior king Nimrod had the power to rule." Quinton "Oh, that is something to think about" and we finished our conversation.

The San People

Louis Liebenberg, in *The Art of Tracking: The Origin of Science*, writes about primitive man:

> A period of hundreds of thousands of years culminated in some of the most important adaptations of the human species: hunting and gathering. From

these adaptation comes much of our intellect, emotions, and basic social life. Only the last ten thousand years have seen the development of an agricultural way of life, and there is no evidence of significant biological change during that period. In order, therefore, to understand the origin and nature of modern human behavior (and the human intellect in particular), we need to understand the evolution of hunter-gatherer subsistence and what mankind lost becoming a hunter warrior (Babel the warrior king Nimrod).

We want to show that in our pursuit of a "better life," however you may define it, we tend to look toward the future, to things not yet extant, for solutions and answers, when much of what we seek might already be there, in the footprints we have left behind. We will borrow the words of another knowledgeable and greatly convinced voice, Laurence van der Post, to highlight something seemingly universal.

> *To me Laurence, it was simply that the older I got, the more and more I felt that we had lost; there was a bushman in everybody, and we'd lost contact with that side of ourselves, and we must learn again from the bushman, to find out what is that inside about. I thought how strange it was that people were digging up old ruins—archaeologists excavating to find out what archaic man was like, and here he was walking about in our midst. Why didn't we ask him? That really is at the back of it: the fact that the bushman personified an aspect of natural man which we all have, but with which we've increasingly lost contact, and that has impoverished us and endangered us … Because I found that the difference between this naked little man in the desert who owned nothing and us was that he is, and we have but no longer are. We have. We've exchanged having for being … And that's what I've tried, merely tried, to bring back—to use him as a bridge between the world in the beginning, with which we've lost touch, and the now.*

The place is Chelsea, England. The year is 1994. An interviewer sits across from a man in the twilight of his eighty-seven years of life. In the tone of his answer is something of a plea that we learn from a people who had, many decades earlier, captured his imagination by showing him something of the illusive fuller self. "The essence of this being (of the Bushmen), I believe, was his sense of belonging: belonging to nature, the universe, life, and his own humanity. He had committed himself utterly to nature as a fish to the sea. He had no sense whatsoever of property, owned no animals, and cultivated no land. Life and nature owned all, and he accepted without question that, provided he was obedient to the urge of the world within him, the world without, which was not separate in his spirit, would provide. How right he was is proved by the fact that nature was kinder to him by far than civilization ever was. This feeling of belonging set him apart from us on the far side of the deepest divide in the human spirit."

The edited excerpt above comes from the book *Testament to the Bushman* by Jane Taylor and Laurens van der Post. It appears as the closing chapter under the title "Witness to a Last Will of Man," and is, perhaps, van der Post's most impassioned writing about the San. Laurens van der Post wore numerous titles in his long life. He was a farmer, educator, explorer, conservationist, journalist, philosopher, and writer. There was something about these hunter-gatherers, a culture that is thought to be more than sixty thousand to eighty thousand years old that so fundamentally touched van der Post.

On our door step is the example, a living culture that still operates from the wisdom of polarity: an ancient way of being that has not made the leap to separation; one that defines itself through being part of everything, rather than making meaning of the self by claiming what it is not. And so, the San look at themselves as a part of the entire world. I am that I am.

Lessons in wisdom and knowing the bushman and other indigenous people can teach us; if we are prepared to listen to what they have to offer:

- Collective healing.
- Knowledge of nutrition's and medical plants.
- Living in harmony with the environment.
- A precise weather forecast six to twelve month ahead.
- Communication of the individual's perception of the truth.
- Situational leadership, masters in surviving.
- Peace through sharing wealth.

Story 13: The Power of the Truth, the feeling of belonging

Creating a feeling that binds and motivates people through creating meaning.

> The head office of an organization sends its marketing staff to visit its subsidiaries, showing them volumes of statistics, such as SWOT and PESTLE analyses, that were used to determine and justify an impossible-to-achieve budget for their next financial year, for this specific subsidiary. How many times does a general manager or director accept a budget when he or she knows the facts are inaccurate and the budget is unachievable? Would it not be in everyone's interest for the manager to stand his or her ground by not accepting the budget, given his or her knowledge of the local markets, the local environment, and the quality of the products and the knowledge and expertise of the local organization? This specific director invited the marketing staff to assist in realizing the budget in the year to come. He asked the headquarters' employees for help.

The director was not able to commit to the targets that had been put together for his local organization; he could not realize the budgets with his crew. The marketing manager from HQ said that that was not their responsibility. The director answered, "Then I will send you a budget that I myself, and my crew can commit to."

Through this action, the manager is avoiding these possibilities:

- The organization undergoing a year of pain as it increasingly realizes that the budget is unachievable.
- Having to manage the expectations of an irate board of directors.
- Generating negative energy when they realize them self's the budget is unrealistic. This also eliminates the inevitable negative corridor conversations that would have gone with this, destroying the morale in the company and destroying the manager's levels of trust with his staff.

The director has liberated his organization and staff, who can then achieve the more realistic goal. Although, initially, the head office may summon this regional director to appear before the executive board to explain his actions, they will ultimately come to appreciate the regional director's honesty and accurate assessment of the situation.

This story is moving beyond old patterns of conditioning, stigmatization, false beliefs, and fear. Every individual involved has the opportunity to become a fuller person, passionate and trusting the others. Why? Because the feeling is okay, understanding of the reality is there.

A simple technique to have a personal answer on the question, is the feeling okay, or is my decision okay?

- Breath in deeply, ask the question ......
- Breath out, an answer comes inside you immediately as : Yes or No

It is as if the answer comes from nowhere, amazingly the answer is, if you do it properly, always correct. In every difficult situation you engage, first breath in—before you give a reaction or comment. Most of the time it is our thinking mind, the echo of the ego, giving an immediate reaction that forces us to convince the other person or the collective. Duality starts; I am right - you are wrong. But we need dialogue in harmony.

Meaning Phase: 5 - Enlightenment

Enlightenment. It is the process of balance between thinking, feeling and inner knowing, a rational mirroring of the self, a process of reconciliation. It is reflection in action once the light within is accepted, it can turn outward to the world. Objective judgment and reflection enables you to let go of the past, to open space for new beginnings, reconciliation. If feeling starts becoming meaning, the feeling creates an unshakable belief in the future and gives the individual and society purpose. It allows the organization to settle down.

Enlightenment is the process of balance between the thinking mind and the inner knowing, a rational mirroring of the self, a process of reconciliation. Once the light within is accepted, it can turn outward to the world. It enables you to let go of the past, to open space for new beginnings. If feeling becomes meaning, the feeling creates an unshakable belief in the future and gives a person purpose.

First we have to answer the question: Why are leaders/managers so afraid of an Encounter? Why can't we change our false beliefs, instead of falling again and again into the same trap!

It is important to know where our false beliefs, fears and conditioners are coming from, because they block us from becoming a beacon of light to inspire other people. Can it be that they are coming or rooted in the story of Babel, the kingdom of duality, fear and warriors?

Duality by Klaus Elle

Story 14: The Tower of Babel

Some belief systems claim this as an actual historical moment, others regard it as fable, and some reject it altogether. Regardless, it is a good metaphor for the point in time when we took our first steps in duality. Farming became an innovation creating a demand for owning land. The city of Babel is supposed to have been the source of laws, wars, empires, kingdoms, countries, religions, ideologies and military hierarchical organization structures. It is this story that illustrates how humanity turned its back on unity (source) by making a temple of duality against polarity. The world was in unity; the people were together inside of one language and consciousness. But then the logic of separation was embraced. The Hunter-Gatherer, once the cornerstone of society, shifted his energy, altering his connection to the world and became a Hunter-Warrior. He changed from the role of provider to the role of conqueror.

The model of the Hunter-Warrior

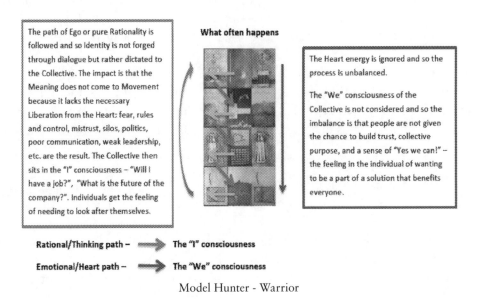

The path of Ego or pure Rationality is followed and so Identity is not forged through dialogue but rather dictated to the Collective. The impact is that the Meaning does not come to Movement because it lacks the necessary Liberation from the Heart: fear, rules and control, mistrust, silos, politics, poor communication, weak leadership, etc. are the result. The Collective then sits in the "I" consciousness – "Will I have a job?", "What is the future of the company?". Individuals get the feeling of needing to look after themselves.

What often happens

The Heart energy is ignored and so the process is unbalanced.

The "We" consciousness of the Collective is not considered and so given imbalance is that people are not given the chance to build trust, collective purpose, and a sense of "Yes we can!" – the feeling in the individual of wanting to be a part of a solution that benefits everyone.

Rational/Thinking path – ⟹ The "I" consciousness

Emotional/Heart path – ⟹ The "We" consciousness

Model Hunter - Warrior

It is important here to note that just as the hunter-warrior model is out of balance, if the "we" consciousness is dominant the individual can be overpowered by the desire of the group. Let us call this the messenger-warrior model. This would be the above diagram in reverse. The messenger-warrior model includes those collectives that are driven by blind faith in dogma, religion, nationalism, and collectivist ideologies (e.g. communism, capitalism, socialism) and so on. This is important to note because it highlights the pervasiveness of duality and how it is damaging toward both the individual and collective even though there may be an illusion of one or the other being a "winner." Might it be this was, approximately five thousand years ago, the fundament for our fear losing the control over farmland and separation in farmland owning tribes?

Tower of Babel an Eye-Opener

The Tower of Babel story in the Bible isn't just about the development of language and the splitting up of mankind. Language was really just a symptom of how mankind slipped into a lower state of consciousness that is based on the ego-centered brain. Most people use the left side of their brains. This state of mind created the civilizations that we have had for the past five thousand years. In addition to emergence of language and the splitting up of mankind, there was the emergence of writing, laws, wars, kingdoms, empires, countries, religions, ideologies, and other hierarchies. There is another group who believe that the Tower of Babel story is about extraterrestrials coming down and genetically engineering mankind, but that is a materialistic interpretation, and the important thing is the mind, not the DNA. What is the point about the Tower of Babel? It's about the state of mankind that has existed since written history and farming started. Nimrod was also the first political leader who was in charge of an army, and every political leader that has existed since him has been in charge of an army as well, to protect their land. Think of any leader we have had throughout history; they have all been hunter warriors. There are very few exceptions, such as Jesus, Mohammed, Buddha, and Gandhi; it is hard to think of any others.

Harmony

It is clear to me that we need a peaceful marriage or reintegration between the hunter-gatherer and the hunter-warrior, and out of this marriage will grow the spirit of goodness over materialism and selfishness. The hunter-gatherer lives in polarity (cultures in harmony next to each other and in tune with all there is, worshipping nature). The hunter-warrior lives in duality (cultures in separation with each other and worshipping the material). As Thich Nhat Hanh said, "We are here to awaken from the illusion of our separateness."

Little faith is required to open the door to create greater possibilities of wellbeing. Just crossing the bridge reveals a higher level of consciousness. We have to develop a different perspective on our beliefs and free ourselves from our basic instincts. The belief systems of today also found their roots in the philosophies of Machiavelli, Descartes and Darwin, suiting the warrior kings who want to stay in power.

Some modern false beliefs:

Descartes' 'I think therefore I am' represents Ego and Rationality with the outcome that the rational ego becomes disconnected from the inner self.

Darwin's evolution theory is characterized as a survival struggle of the fittest, the dominance of the ego.

The term Machiavellianism is defined as: 'The political doctrine of Machiavelli … [which] denies the relevance of morality in political affairs and holds that craft and deceit are justified in pursuing and maintaining political power.' This definition implies that in the arena of power the end justifies the means. This is essentially the core of Machiavellianism.

The questions we should ask ourselves:

Is our destiny to remain stuck in duality and fear-bound behavior?

OR

Can we really work together in harmony in diversity and so, sustain collective prosperity and meaning?

What is needed for welfare?

A 'Thought', the seed planted in the fertile soil of our souls that provokes meaning.

Story 15: A thought, the seed for reconciliation

South Africa went through the process of awareness and reconciliation that has become known as the peaceful transformation of the Rainbow Nation. It seems however, that now the vision of the Rainbow Nation has been lost in a climate of fear and division. Fear creates the need for control and leaders who deal in fear will manufacture crises and even wars to maintain their control.

However, South Africa has not yet started with the process of forgiveness necessary to liberate the Collective. If South Africa is truly able to unite its people into a rainbow nation, it has the potential of becoming a living leadership school for the world.

Imagine how this could create a major new wisdom industry that would generate employment and welfare, both within and outside of South Africa. Not to separate people, but to bring them together. This is true equality. If South Africa could harness these powers, it could stand as a role model for the world. If it could let go of the past and liberate itself from the stigmatizing idea of the politicians that its people are disadvantaged, the country could become a beacon of light to the world. Imagine what the world would look like if we invested in humanity instead of materialism, where people from a highly industrialized world, who are stressed and desperately need healing, could come to centers of Embracing Leadership in South Africa.

Story 16: Reconciliation in a working environment.

At the Rio Tinto Palabora Mining Company in late 2011, the managing director had to address all of the 3800 employees in his introduction to the post- LeKgotla process. The managing director had this to say:

> The mining industry worldwide has a management history that has resulted in a significant communication gap between the executives, office staff, and workers. The culture has been one in which management groups believe they hold the best information and knowledge and that workers should, for the most part, follow their instructions. In our rapidly changing world, we are seeing the collapse of hierarchical approaches in favor of flatter and more open and embracing leadership.

> It has become essential for leaders to develop a good understanding of the collective culture of the majority of people in the business in order to identify talent, skills, and aspirations. This is essential to ensure the right people are in the right jobs to implement the business vision and thereby allow companies to progress and achieve new levels of prosperity.

> This means, in order to progress and improve, we must break the historical chains that have bound us while not destroying our roots. To achieve this, dialogue is a very powerful ally and must be mastered. Dialogue cuts through the constraints that bind a company and promotes understanding and peace.

> So enlightenment, bringing the light on our own judgments, creates space for accepting the other person and therefore can rediscover unity. The general manager of human resources echoed these words:

> "In my thirty-year career in human resources, I have come across a number of initiatives aimed at changing culture, influencing behavior, and motivating people. What surprises me is that most of the initiatives focused on what the organization can do and not necessarily on gaining the understanding of what the people think it should be."

The dialogue process creates an opportunity for everyone to participate and make a contribution, and it gives the leader the right to make decisions that are embraced by all. This is a powerful way of legitimizing leadership. This leadership privilege does not come cheap, as it requires the leadership to be authentic, vulnerable, and collaborative. When one person can see the light, it shines over all the others as seen here in a LeKgotla gathering.

Morning Ritual
"Good morning, chief. For me, this LeKgotla process had more of a psychological effect, because when I came to the Kgotla there were issues that I was scared to share with you. But when I saw all the managers prepared to listen to our problems, for the first time, I had hope that this company is moving forward. I would like to say to everyone in leadership positions that you, chief, came at the right time because the company was going down. My prayer today is that God gave you the wisdom and courage to make the Palabora Company work."

Perhaps most significantly, the employee addressed the entire leadership of the company—no longer afraid of claiming his right to speak—suggesting that this new energy may even receive the blessing of God (the light inside you) as well as the gift of wisdom (not expected) to "make the Palabora Company work". This is the logic of unlocking the inner knowing of individuals inside of a collective. The unexpected result is the full benefit of their collective energy and wisdom. He concluded with the following:

The stories and metaphors in this book are a testament to an organization tapping into people's wisdom and knowing. When the collective is connected with each other to deliver value for the benefit of all. If you want to get the organization talking, allow space for listening without prejudice. In this way, you are able to dig deep into the mind of human ability.

The outcome of the Rio Tinto LeKgotla is a good example of dialogue:

- 3,800 voices voicing their voice,
- 520 ideas,
- 60 root causes,
- 9 themes
- 35 decisions.

A collective about achieving the best possible result to the benefit of the entire collective and individuals, is identity that has meaning made manifest.

In an environment of honesty and trust and the absolute belief that from unity, diversity and harmony comes the feeling and understanding: I am because we are. Working in an environment characterized by dialogue is the right way. It is very important in society that their leaders also accept and listen to the shadows. As a leader, make the collective aware, through understanding, the importance of the voices of the shadows.

We can identify three levels of shadows in organizations or ourselves. They are the wanderers, the avengers, and the witches. If management does not accept wanderers, wanderers try to enter the clan by expressing and explaining their positive criticism. Once they fail in explaining their perceptions of the reality, they become avengers; skeptical people who try to let the team fail or who are unhelpful. If they continuously fail to access the clan, they become witches and try to break down the structures of the pyramid/hierarchy of the organization. They become cynical and, ultimately, will be excluded from the organization permanently. In the Lekgotla, dialogue the leader will include the negative powers of the shadow of fear. He will first consult the witches, then the avengers, and then the wanderers before talking to the clan and the egos in the organization. The messengers are important in filtering skepticism and cynicism within the organization. This can also result in a turnaround in the way the witches, avengers, and wanderers work. In the Lekgotla [encounter], the leader will include the negative powers of the shadow of fear. Their joint energy will unlock positive energy and include those who operate in the shadow of fear [as] they have the important mirroring function of a different view.

Story 17: A Lesson from my Father

There is a wonderful experience I want to share with you about reconciliation and awareness and the shadow of collective belief.

"On the other side of the border are living bad people" was the general public opinion in 1947. This story is about acceptance, forgiveness, reconciliation, light, and unity in diversity.

When my father returned in August 1945 from being a prisoner of war in Germany, I got the fright of my life. He was dressed in a way that I took him to be a ghost. I remember, jumping on the bed shouting at him, "Go away! Go away!"

"I am your father, don't be afraid," were the words that came back at me. My mother had to calm me while he left the room.

A year later, my father invited me for a cycling tour, and we crossed the border post in the city of Coevorden, where I was born, into Germany. We ended up in a small farming village called Emlichheim. It was here that he wanted to teach me an important lesson.

"You see, here on the other side of the border are living human beings like you and me," he said.

This man, who had experienced things at the hands of the German war machine, was now preaching reconciliation, forgiveness, and tolerance—unity in diversity. It seemed he had long ago forgiven his captors. Had he seen the light in himself? Had it something to do with the beautiful name we are carrying, de Liefde, that translates to "love"? I think that my father's understanding of unity in diversity and the always-positive caring of my mother have been with me my whole life. I thank them for giving me life.

Learning through introspection, we can understand our conditioners and the influence on our physical body, mind, and soul. This understanding is important when the collective starts the difficult process of reconciliation. All of the talents of the trinity of leadership are needed.

ULC- quote:
'The ego is a restricted energy. When the physical body dies, the ego dies. Soul energy is unrestricted energy. When the body dies; the soul goes back into the ocean of awareness, infinity'. (A scientific example of this is the fact that the human body loses twenty-one grams at the moment of death.)

The ego energy is able to reduce the potential of our soul energy. In order to grow in this lifetime, one needs to give space to the soul energy. Empty your 'Babylon' memory box, your 'Babbel' box of the mind. The mind's ego dream can act as a barrier or conditioner for our inner knowing to flourish. It prevents our physical body, mind, and soul from coming into balance. This mind's thinking dream is, in 90 percent of the cases, your wrong advisor, the ego pursuing a person to put more effort in a certain direction such as; you must become a manager, a doctor and so on. But he or she never arrives at the dream's end station, and it exhausts a person as it drains energy from following a false belief.

Ego has become master to the soul rather than a partner (tool, enabler, support) for it. The question in life is how to peel off the layers of accumulated conditioning. This is only possible if you know who you are. The maturation of ULC leadership navigator will be explained in the following chapters and is a guide for understanding who you really are. Answering the key question of how to open the talents of the "I" in the domain of the "We."

In his book *Fate into Destiny*, Robert Ohotto writes, "In other words, coming to terms with something also transforms Self Fate into Destiny." It was only when he chose to heed the voice of destiny that he began to heal. This story will resonate with most of us because we'll all encounter a situation where creativity of our soul begins to knock on the door of our ego. And if we don't invite that part of us into the ego as a noble guest, we'll also meet fate. I like Robert Ohotto suggestion: Invite the noble guest.

$\mathcal{10}$ Meaning Phase: 6 - Liberation

Liberation. A real liberation can only be there when real forgiving has taken place. Forgiving is only possible by making peace with the past: patterns, conditioning, blockages, and associated fear are reduced. This is key to cementing the meaning that inspires and drives action; Forgiving is liberation in practice. But first, let us take a step back to read the story of the incubator so we understand the importance of the energy flows through the ULC and the role each part (Not expected, Encounter, and so on) plays in both the Individual and Collective. Liberation is the step from reconciliation to forgiving oneself and the other. It is an explosion of a positive energy of trust, opening the doors for a caring and passionate Collective. People are inspired, new concepts will emerge. Liberation is the final result of the thought manifested in a vision by a passionate Collective.

Story 18: The Incubator, letting go of the past.

It is the early 1990s. The Dutch government made the decision to implement a cut in the healthcare budget and expenditure by 25 percent. Being the last quarter of the financial year, the news sends waves through the market. The companies in the medical-supplies industry are greatly affected by this, as this period generally accounts for around 40 percent of their annual income. Panic hangs in the air. The director of one such company approaches his friend, a philosopher and astrologer, to discuss what might be done in response. Some of the director's competitors are responding by giving huge discounts to their customers in an effort to and reduce stock volumes and bring in much-needed income. The director, however, is not prepared to follow the same path. A feeling in his heart says that this is wrong: "I could have done this yesterday or six months ago; why do I need a disaster to give a discount?"

They discuss the matter in detail. The philosopher has an idea. The company should to set up a meeting with the hospital staff (doctors, nurses, administration officials, purchasing departments, etc.), all of those who will be most affected.

Such a dialogue, he suggests, could revolve around talking about the collective pain that is being felt throughout the entire value chain because of the spending cuts. The director agrees. The arrangements are made.

On the day of the meeting, the philosopher is the first speaker. "Do you know who you are?" he asks, "And why you are in this situation"? The unexpected: Without wanting an answer, he drops a bomb. He gives a definition of the role and place of medical healthcare employees: "You are the rubbish dump of the health industry!" Instead of being healers, as these people understand themselves, he suggests that they are responsible for managing the rubbish dump that is their position in the health sector. His explanation is that they are being governed by an increasing number of rules and procedures, passed down by people in faraway offices who have little practical knowledge of what goes into the job of providing health care. The present situation is a good example. With increasing demand for healthcare services by a growing population, the cuts are putting pressure on the resources, equipment, and staff available to meet the demand. Simply put, the impact of the cuts will be felt by healthcare professionals and their patients, not by those responsible for cutting budgets.

The philosopher continues. To add more salt to the collective wound, healthcare professionals do not have a platform or opportunity to comment or give feedback on their situation to the powers that be. "You are voiceless!" He ends his speech. "But the director has a solution for you." The comment stirs the room. But the biggest surprise is reserved for the director who knows nothing of this. What solution? He rises from his seat nervously. Nervous feet search for courage as they shuffle slowly across the stage toward the microphone. Then it comes—a thought.

"We are all in the same boat together." The director said to the audience. "Importantly, we all need to keep our energy up and stay positive. I have a thought." There is a shift in the mood in the room. Hope? "Instead of keeping stockpiles of incubators in the warehouse, why don't we use this equipment, sending it home with the mothers of premature babies? If we show these mothers how to use the incubators properly, we will empower them to return home with their babies earlier than usual, where they will be able to look after their newborns on their own." He continues—energy building around the thought. "In practice, we need the commitment of you doctors and nurses. If you give some of your free time, and we supply the equipment, together we can train the mothers. The result will be that some of the pressure will be removed from you in the hospitals. It will also bring back meaning in your work as healers, and it will create a different kind of interaction and relationship with those we are caring for."

Collectively, there is agreement. The collective audience returns to their places of work, and the action around the thought begins. The beauty of this thought was that it spoke to, and so united, people working in the hospitals and their supplier across the value chain. The healthcare provider was united inside of a new and different collective with a single mission of better serving those who needed them. It created a new sense of purpose and energy despite the difficulty of the times. More than this, the beneficiaries of this care also became a part of this collective, as they were now invited to be a part of the process. They were no longer patients; they became partners.

The delivery of a "total solution" took on a different value. The company's competitors could not understand it: even with discounts, their products were less attractive. The long-term impact was that hospitals decided that their preferred supplier would be the company that really cared for people. The whole idea, from start to finish, was about people and finding a solution that was the best for all.

A simple idea, when acted on with feeling, is able to give the people involved a renewed sense of identity and meaning. When people gather around an identity that has a clear purpose, it has the effect of creating meaning. The result is that a new collective is formed. Individuals accept the vision or goal within themselves and are prepared to contribute their ideas, talents, and energy to realize a common goal as a collective. In this sense, it becomes a cycle of collective prosperity.

The Incubator story is a good example of starting with a thought and going through the two phases and six intersections of the life cycle.

The explanation of the ULC- process flow (roadmap):

Phase I – Identity

1. Not Expected
   The not expected sparked the thought of the director on phase: "Incubators and premature babies go home with their mothers." What happened here was that the thought was the spark of a new identity or innovation that became a light at the end of the tunnel? There was a sense of wisdom in the thought because it was to the benefit of everyone in the value chain (producer, service provider, end user) at a time when everyone was demotivated and despairing.

2. Encounter

   People gathered in dialogue with the thought—which provides discussion and commitment in support of the idea. What happened here was people encountered one another in dialogue on how the thought could become reality. People needed to engage with this new, potential identity. The growing, positive feeling in the people was the beginning of a new collective identity in healthcare with all the stakeholders involved. The result was an understanding: we are all in this together, united or divided.

3. Transformation

   People return to their workplaces and begin to see how the thought will become a reality—what it will look like in practice. What happened here was the new awareness that the thought was in everyone's best interests; a sense of passion and motivation in a previously depressed environment emerged. The transformation, energetically, was the creation of a genuine sense of caring for people in the healthcare sector: "We care about people" became the provider's phrase.

Identity is a strong energy that binds individuals together and limits fear. It is the first fundamental step to sustainability, cooperation, and unity of purpose. This phase paves the way for transformation toward meaning.

Phase II – Meaning

4. Movement

   People begin to put the thought in practice, and there is action around making the idea a reality. What happened here was that the new feeling created the drive to do, the beginning of meaning. The feeling of joy in the moment and the sense of purpose and mutual trust (unity) allowed the people to make peace with the current situation; they were liberated from their fear of tough times. The result was a relieving or welcoming state of affairs. In essence, people found their power as they saw they were able to do something, which fostered a sense of purpose (e.g. doctors and nurses giving their time, training people on how to use the equipment, etc.).

5. Enlightenment

   People feel a new sense of meaning. They were inspired. It activated their thinking and inner knowing; they were able to see their own light. The healthcare employees rediscovered the love and passion for caring for people, which gave a sense of meaning in their lives. It was a form of reconciliation and objective judgment.

6. Liberation
    People feel a sense of release from past concerns about budgets and rules and the reality of difficult times. What happened people carried the 'thought' that it was possible to manage reduced budgets and strict rules as well as give the best possible care for people within the limitations. People are forgiving of themselves in this situation; they no longer play the victim of the selfish. This had the effect of creating new awareness, helping transformation, and unlocking a positive feeling to manifest the thought: Yes, we can!

    Identity and Meaning are the foundation for sustainability in practice. It acts as the glue to bind individuals together inside a collective by unlocking the essence of life, fueling the energy of passion and motivation and revealing the beauty of life. People started forming a new collective.

The story presented here, many would agree, is an unusual one. At its most simple, it is a story of unlocking and nurturing the leadership potential in each individual inside of a Collective. The Director's idea, being grounded in a concern for the wellbeing of everyone, and not just his company, resulted in a widespread, sustainable economic model. By changing the environment in the healthcare sector at that period in time he facilitated a process of new manifestation (action), inside a climate of harmony, and in a way the idea was carried by the people (company staff, healthcare workers, patients).

This is a story of transcendence. It is a metaphor for moving beyond old patterns of conditioning, stigmatization, false beliefs, and fear, so that every individual involved can become a fuller person through:

- Being part of decisions taken (Identity),
- Feeling a sense of belonging (Meaning),
- Being trusted, relied upon, and responsible for sharing the best of their unique talents by making contribution to the creation of collective good fortune (Collective).

The result is unity of purpose, passion for work, and prosperity; all of which reduces the need for rules of bureaucracy.

The key question is this: How do you open up the talents of the "I" in the domain of the "We"? Are there guidelines for passing the barriers of reconciliation, let go of the past, and forgive?

Reconciliation and Forgiveness

Let's reflect for a moment on the process of reconciliation and forgiveness, as mentioned in the story above.

The tragedy of today is that we don't seem to want to learn from the ancient peoples and cultures that understand balance, reconciliation, and forgiveness in practice. They have bequeathed to us much wisdom and plenty of warnings—what to do and what not to do. Through their deeper wisdom, they support the full development of the individual that benefits the collective. Inside this wisdom they then gather together in dialogue (Lekgotla) and the solutions as are carried by the people (organization/society). Their understanding of life means that they are healthy in their soul, mind and body, not suffering from the many ailments and sicknesses of the so-called modern human: stress and burnout. For individuals, reconciliation is the process of creating space and making good with another person. However, the danger of reconciliation is that a person's anger may remain and this anger could be activated at any moment by the slightest provocation. Forgiveness is the solution to overcome this.

> Forgiveness therefore requires forgiving oneself first. Only then can forgiving of the other person take place. If the individual does not forgive him or herself first, the guilt and anger remain, feeding the ego and creating fear or dominance in the individual. The process of letting go can only be done collectively. A Lekgotla's - encounter is very instrumental in the process of forgiving and understanding the other person.

The Paradox

> The paradox in a rational process is that the human being has to go through the process of letting go of the past. If we do not follow that process of letting go very carefully, there is a danger that the strategies will be implemented too quickly. The result will be demotivation, conflict, and fear in the collective. Many people ask the question, "But how do I do this, and how do I know I really forgive the other person?" Your inner knowing has the senses to give the true answer. A helpful method is to sense through breathing and feel in the body what is contained in the words. Is it voice or speech? Voice and speech have a different resonance. It either resonates in the heart or in the mind. This is something that can be practiced in the self as well as used in the observation and interaction with others. It takes some practice to be able to fully listen to yourself and others, but it can be surprisingly accurate.

- Speech in this context is the ability to express thoughts and feelings by articulation. This is the action of putting into words an idea or feeling.
- Voice is the supposed utterance of a guiding spirit, typically giving instruction or advice.
- Sense is a feeling that something is the case, and the body perceives a stimulus.

The Method

Prepare a question. Breathe in and out deeply and ask yourself the question while in the process of breathing. Questions:

- Shall I stop my cooperation with Mr. So and So or that organization
- Is the proposed reorganization the proper solution
- Is divorce an option

The answer comes immediately sensed as yes or no in your body.

1. Wrong solution resonate in the mind with: No
2. Good or right solution resonates in the heart with: Yes

For the fundamental question of do I forgive myself or the other person, the answer is immediately there; even if you want to fake a yes while it is no, your whole body senses it is no. Explore your inner guide. Try it; it is just one breath away. The aligning of the thought, feeling, and thinking mind (our ego) is where the invisible work actually happens, for if these are balanced, then we as individuals or collective will come into being, having purpose in life which allow them to forgive. This results in a strong identity and meaning in life.

The experience will be clear:

- "Every day of my life is one of joy."
- "When the community is healed, we as individuals are healed in the process."
- "We embracing the I."
- "People are liberated from the past; as a collective they can move forward to a future of new beginnings."

Take a reflective moment and look to the words of the Universal Life Cycle. What are these words meaning for you?

I - Identity	1- Not Expected Thought Wisdom	2- Encounter Senses Understanding	3- Transformation Awareness Knowledge	Inspiring Spiral spirit energy
II - Meaning	4- Movement Feeling Mercy	5- Enlightenment Reconciliation Judgment	6- Liberation Forgiveness Beauty	Passion Soul energy
III - Collective	7- Community Manifest Eternity	8- Embracement We Foundation	9- Full ending Abundance Kingdom	Unconditional love Infinity energy

Still we can read the stories, the recommendations. The question remains, what to do in the daily practice of life? The logic that works so simply through the artwork, the etchings in different colors, the etched plates, evades description in words. The artwork is instrumental in assisting leaders and individuals in exposing themselves to the members of a collective / organization or society.

Quote: Lucy Maud Montgomery

> "There is so much in the world for all of us if we only have the eyes [thought] to see it, and the heart [feeling] to love it, and the hand [manifest] to gather it to ourselves".

Phase II: Meaning roadmap for creating purpose and letting go of the past
Is the process of awareness - reconciliation and forgiveness?

A- the thinking side **B- the feeling side**

Step 4

Liberation—*Beauty*	4) Movement—*Mercy*	7) Liberation—*Beauty*
Individuals committed to make tangible results. The logic of Empowerment inspires the individuals to work together. Physical preparation the mental and emotional acceptance of the new strategy. A	People starting to realize what has to be done. Awareness develops for the responsibility to perform as collective. Convert identity into meaning that resonates in the heart of the crew (individuals). A positive feeling develops. The restructuring takes place.	Preparation mentally and emotionally for the acceptation of the current situation. Creating a climate of trust that reduces fear. B

Step 5

3) Not Expected—*Wisdom*	5) Enlightenment—*Judgment*	17) Not Expected—*Wisdom*
The capability creating the space for an awakening. The wisdom of the vision becomes logic for the Individual. A	Objective judgement of the vision/idea. Distancing from the past. Belief in the future, vision carried by the people. Use the light within. Process of letting go of the past *The power of reconciliation.* *Passing second barrier*	Empty the conscious mind's memory box of fear for the future. Growing feeling of self-confidence. B

Step 6

Transformation—*Knowledge*	6) Liberation —*Beauty*	Transformation—*Knowledge*
The individual moves away from defensiveness towards a proactive attitude, implementing the new strategy. Individual commitment to realize the vision/plans/ideas. A	Empowering, liberated from the past. The noble guest of forgiveness knocks on the door of the thinking mind. People are inspired and passionate, there is purpose in their work *Passing third barrier*	People's resistance to transformation and fear for change is dramatically reduced. It is replaced by a positive feeling of having meaning in work. The feeling: "Yes we can" B

Story 19: Sharing the Truth

A Managing Director decided to hold a Lekgotla with his staff because he had become aware that gossip was rife in the corridors and common areas of the company. This is demotivating the employees and the collective motivation and productivity was declining. An employee requests that the truth of the situation be addressed. The Director responded that in a Lekgotla every participant has the fundamental right to voice his meaning or perception of the gossiping problem.

The truth emerges: the management team has divided into two groups, with four members of the management team of seven always staying together, two members of the team staying outside this group and one neutral, sometimes in sometimes out. The two members that are always together often publicly complain that their four colleagues do not invite them to join for social gatherings after working ours. This has split the workforce into two camps. The Director confirms the truth to the Collective. Two groups were formed, one group representing the management team and the second representing the staff. They are given two hours to come up with practical solution. With the truth on the table, the open atmosphere of trust unlocks the wisdom within. Firstly, to appoint the receptionist as 'The Truth Lady' most of the gossiping was ventilated to her. People perceived her as a wise and trustful person.

The decision was taken to appoint her as 'Trust Lady' and officially publish in their company magazine, with her responsibilities. She was a wise woman, similar to the story of "the bratwurst lady". Secondly the management team is reorganized. One of the 'outsiders' leaves the company and the other, who had not been happy in her position, assigned a different role. After sharing the truth in the Lekgotla, the company begins to flourish once again. Meaning was back and this changed the climate on the work floor to, united we are strong. Communication dramatically improved.

If we all have the courage to expose ourselves to the collective, we create a climate of trust. We allow ourselves to explore our wisdom inside, and we can link our inner knowing to our conscious knowledge, creating interaction between objective knowledge and subjective knowledge. The ULC does not solve problems; only people who have an attitude of willingness can do so. It puts words to realities and creates a blueprint, a road map, for the way forward. It is a tool that nurtures change; it does not reveal anything new, uncovering, instead, truths and answers that were already there, sometimes dormant.

It unlocks -the universe within- energy in every individual. It is not an external solution but rather a key to help unlock your inner knowing and wisdom. It is holistic in that it does not address one element or aspect of the individual or organization/society; instead, it looks at the individual in his or her entirety so that what is uncovered or learned can be used for the betterment of life and the community.

As a collective and individual we can start to execute the principle of awareness, reconciliation and forgiving. Let's rediscover the values of living together in harmony, supporting and thriving from an embracing thought leadership style on the fundamentals of dialogue and our wisdom within.

Meaning: Summary note

A collective that has a strong Identity that is Meaningful is able to work in harmony toward achieving the common goal. Without a meaning carried in the people's hearts, we cannot create a harmonious collective. I want to repeat it again and again, the process of forgiving is fundamental. Liberation is the final step in creating balance in a collective before we start the manifestation of executing the vision in the collective/organization.

An example of how difficult it is for leaders to realize universal liberation and true forgiveness is what happened in South Africa. South Africa went through the process of awareness and reconciliation (truth and reconciliation commission) that has become known as the peaceful transformation of the "Rainbow Nation" (which Nelson Mandela talked about), but it has not yet started with the process of forgiveness, and this is a necessary step to liberate the collective. It seems, however, the vision of the Rainbow Nation has been lost in a climate of fear and division. Fear creates the need for control, and leaders who deal in fear will manufacture crises and even wars to maintain their control.

After such a period of fundamental change, you can expect uncertainty, fear for the future, duality and so on. After a visionary leader like Mandela, there is need for messenger/hunter energy a leader whom: Can act as a steward for reconciliation and forgiveness. The custodian of the truth and living together, in South Africa's case black, white and colored in harmony. This leader makes clear what kind of commitment is needed and what has to be done to realize the vision. They understand that a sustainable future can only be achieved through forgiving. This is on ongoing process of realignment and dialogue.

MEANING is the foundation for sustainability in practice. It acts as the glue to bind individuals together inside a collective by unlocking the essence of life, creating the energy of passion, motivation, and revealing the beauty of life.

4-Movement	5-Enlightenment	6-Liberation
Mercy	Judgment	Beauty
"Yes, we can!" Barack Obama	"Our deepest fear is not that we are inadequate. Our deepest fear is that we are powerful beyond measure. It is our light, not our darkness that most frightens us … And as we let our own light shine, we unconsciously give other people permission to do the same. As we are liberated from our own fear, our presence automatically liberates others." Marianne Williamson	"We can easily forgive a child who is afraid of the dark. The real tragedy of life is when men are afraid of the light." Plato

// Collective Phase

Collective: Collective is the last phase of the ULC, consisting of the three intersections: Community - Embracement – Full Ending.

Community

There is alignment between the thought and feeling (identity and meaning) that binds the collective and creates the energy needed to realize the vision tangibly. Without this balance, both in the individual and collective, manifesting the vision becomes difficult. What happens is that a new community is born as the result of having a purpose!

Embracement

The collective is bound together in practice as individuals drive the vision to completion in their own unique ways, by taking responsibility for their contributions. They start to develop the new strategies needed when the not expected might happens. Each person can see the vision as well as his or her role in the community. The risk is that people get into a routine, arrogance of we are the best, the strongest can develop a behavior of dominance. This can undo the entire process.

Full ending

There is balance between heart and mind, matter and spirit—polarity. The past is being put to rest. Energetically then, the cycle comes to completion; there is a release. The cycle provides that which is needed for the next level of prosperity. When this balance exists, a new cycle of prosperity can start at a higher awareness level

The ULC as a Diagnostic Tool for Organizations

From the stories, we have learnt that the problems lie in the Identity, Meaning or Collective. To solve the issues we need embracing leadership and awareness about our reality. The recipe is always an energy mix, a cocktail of trust, thoughts and belief in your inner knowing as well perceptions, sharing knowledge and passion. The alignment of the different individual perceptions of the issues can only be solved through dialogue and visualization of the problems. Most of the time when a collective becomes demotivated, having no success, it is important to know the real cause.

How instrumental is the ULC in this situation? First, if we want to solve the problem, we need to have a diagnosis. In most of the cases we change the conditions and circumstances but not the "CAUSE"! The end result is that nothing is solved and over time the disillusions become even bigger, ending in a worst-case scenario, in a bankrupt company or society.

History gives us the best examples: World War I followed by World War II. After World War 1 only the conditions and circumstances were changed with no change of the cause, leading to war on an even greater scale. The Marshall Plan then helped changed the cause, thought energy.

The question asked: Which ULC images represent the problem/issues in our organization, division or department. The groupings of the selections from the individual attendees can be in the Identity, Meaning or Collective phase. For large gatherings, the selections can be done electronically via mobile phone; "SMS." The outcome is displayed on a screen. Every attendee receives the outcome immediately, for all participants the communication about the result is transparent. The focus of the employees is, without blaming one another, drawn to the issues. Keeps the collective together-oneness. We are all sailing on board of the same ship therefor: "In the same boat".

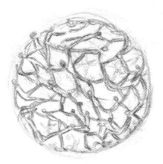

For sustainability the law is: CHANGE THE CAUSE!

Diagnostic tool

Identity	1- *Not Expected* Thought *Wisdom*	2- *Encounter* Senses *Understanding*	3- *Transformation* Awareness *Knowledge*	Inspiring Spiral energy
Meaning	4- *Movement* Feeling *Mercy*	5- *Enlightenment* Reconciliation *Judgment*	6- *Liberation* Forgiveness *Beauty*	Passion Soul energy
Collective	7- *Community* Manifest *Eternity*	8- *Embracement* We *Foundation*	9- *Full ending* Abundance *Kingdom*	Unconditional love Infinity energy

The essence and power of the outcome: The perception of the situation comes from within, displayed to the outside as a selection. The outcome of the selections goes within (reflections) and at the end the proposed solutions, coming from within, are communicated with the Collective; a LeKgotla dialogue.

So Within, so Without

ULC Perception table - WE NEED:

Not expected	Encounter	Transformation
More Wisdom using the power of thought. Sense of the reality.	More Understanding of one another using all our senses	More sharing our Knowledge Awareness for new forms
Movement	Enlightenment	Liberation
More compassion and feeling Reduce fear	More objective Judgment Through reconciliation	More through forgiveness More passion/ trust/new vision
Community	Embracement	Full ending.
More manifesting the vision Better communication. More positive energy and team work	More absolute confidence in the We. To get rid of our Arrogance and gossiping.	More new perspectives, a new phase For growth.

In the Kgotla gathering, The leader selects topics for different workgroups to discuss. The group leader presents a solution back to the attendees. An interesting exercise always is asking the group participants to select, depending on the problem, a colleague as their group's leader. As a leader, can you imagine the power of this working together, based on the perceptions of individuals in a collective whose voices are heard?

Awaken the universe within the collective, accessing their thought power. The power of imagination: A platform for the creation of new forms, carried by the people. What happens here is the subconscious mind comes into action. The individuals inside a collective manifest their individual knowing to (outside) the collective.

If we return to the ULC, we can get a feeling for the qualities of the common when we take the decision to use the Universal Life Cycle as proposed in this book. To put it into practice ourselves. You will have the experience that you are more able to use the lifecycle than you thought. The universal can apply precisely because it makes no claims to the specific. If balance is found and polarity is embraced and acted on, then we will enjoy the fruits that are the power of trinity. If the cycle is navigated inside a relationship of balance, then the flow is seamless, and the picture, when in balance, will be one of harmony, communication, cooperation, prosperity, and sustainability over the long term. This is a healthy collective made up of healthy individuals, where the one contributes and supports the best that is in the other.

Phase III: Collective roadmap for prosperity and sustainability:

A- thinking side **B- feeling side**

Step 7

Community—*Eternity*	7) Community—*Eternity*	Community—*Eternity*
The power of the Individual bonded together. The strategist can explore new horizons. A	Purpose and vision are aligned. The people are passionate to manifest the vision. There is belief in the thought becoming a reality. There is purpose.	Joy, love, companionship. A caring community. People have a strong identity, feeling of belonging and meaning. B

Step 8

Encounter—*Understanding*	8) Embracement—*Foundation*	Encounter—*Understanding*
The Collective understands they have to take full responsibility for their role to contribute. Through understanding, anchoring the new approach inside the collective, the new identity in action. A	A) This is where the true Collective (Individual and Collective) reveals itself and the successes of its efforts are consolidated. Preparing for a new circle of prosperity and new creations of form. Developing a new strategy. Or preparing for the not expected. B) If there is an imbalance here – due to the trap of arrogance and dominance of "we are the best and strongest". Babel effect can lead to a downfall. *Passing the fourth barrier*	Sensing if the forgiving is real. The new awareness emotion in action. Listen if there is fear for the future or dominance of power, the influenza for demotivation. B

Step 9

Full ending—*Kingdom*	9) Full ending—*Kingdom*	Full ending—*Kingdom*
Introspective process of finding any blockages and barriers that might remain that analytically can be solved. This is the finish line. A	The space is cleared for a new cycle. The collective (organization) moves into a new phase of prosperity amplified at a higher conscious level. A new vision can emerge. *Entering a new not expected* - a new cycle. ∞	The ritual burning the past emotionally and mentally is the result of forgiveness. The ritual is part of an introspective process of finding any emotional blockages that might remain. This is the finish line. B

Story 20: The Loss Making Company

A company, a subsidiary of a multinational producing medical equipment, lost money over a three year period. It was a product-oriented company that was in trouble because the market often found the products too expensive. It had to either close down or undergo a major reorganization. The board of directors appointed a new 'chief' to set things right. This chief encountered a negative atmosphere and low confidence in the self. Employees were afraid of the future, felt numb and had an expectant attitude. Even the building mirrored this feeling: it exuded a depressing and negative atmosphere and there were visible signs of a lack of maintenance.

First the chief decided to improve the environment. Using simple means, he refurbished the passageways and toilets. By doing so, he showed that he respected his employees, acknowledged their dignity. In this way he also signaled that people should take personal responsibility for their living and working conditions. Employees were given the opportunity of using a paintbrush on their free Saturday. In contrast to what everyone expected, the 'chief' didn't begin his work by speaking about cutting costs and reorganization; he spoke about providing meaning, respect and sharing the truth.

(Life Cycle: 1. Not Expected) He felt it was necessary to discuss these things in order to create a solid organization. Following the approach of relating to his employees as people, he showed them Jan Montyn's nine etches and asked them to choose the depiction that best suited them as an organization. Surprisingly enough, eight out of ten employees indicated etch nine, which is called "Full Ending". After that they were offered an explanation of the nine themes that make up the constant cycle of life. They then saw that their choice reflected their perception of the situation. By choosing "Full Ending" they reflected the expectation that the company, and therefore their jobs, were ending. The chief posited that "Full Ending" meant something to him. He organized several in depth dialogues on two themes: "What is our identity as a company in the market? What is the meaning of that to us as people?"

These were real "encounters" (Life Cycle: 2. Encounter) between people about giving meaning in work and about the question of their own identity. The encounters took the form of company meetings with groups of fifty people, organized at an outside location on a Friday and Saturday. The fifty employees were a cross-section of the company. These meetings were rounded off with a meeting on a Saturday at the head office, at which all one hundred and fifty employees were present. Afterwards there was also an informal get-together. The skepticism that was certainly present in the beginning, changed during this process into a fundamentally positive attitude, needed for the transformation process.

In the transformation process that followed, the company crossed over from thinking in terms of product to thinking in terms of providing services and education to the market. The motto they had thought up was 'We love people', which was perfectly suited to the selling of medical equipment. The energy released during the dialogues pumped up the process of "transformation" (Life Cycle: 3. Transformation). A new élan was radiated to the outside world and therefore towards the marketplace. Through sharing the truth, mutual trust was restored. In a relatively short time, six months, there was a new climate of collaboration. The crippling fear of retrenchment had disappeared. The company asked for everyone to give of their best – optimum input and creativity – to keep the company afloat in stormy weather.

Based on information gleaned from the various Lekgotla meetings, the chief set a new goal for the employees; to obtain a prestigious client with allure. This would change the company's image. The campaign was given the name "Tour de France". There was no talk of an ultimate goal, just of getting over the Alpe d'Huez – the symbol of one order from a high-profile customer. The entire company accepted the challenge. Everyone started to move. (Life Cycle: 4. Movement) and every person rode in the 'Tour', conscious to perform and manifest the thought. Trust was placed in the director [chief] as pack leader. When the first order was obtained, there was a powerful lobby initiated by the competition in the market to have this order cancelled. Two nerve-wracking weeks ensued during which the order was in danger of being cancelled. But the 'high profile' customer felt more attracted by the vision of the transforming company, and the competition came off second best. Once the threat had disappeared, the company felt for the first time that its problems had been surmounted and that its community once again feels it had control of their own destiny. The metamorphosis was noticed in the marketplace and the first goal was achieved with not one, but three substantial orders from three 'high profile' customers.

The chief allowed the organization to come to rest and consciously decided that the next goal did not have to produce an immediate result. (Life Cycle: 5. Enlightenment). This gave the organization the opportunity to determine its own goals, thrashing them out together as a group. In this way they achieved their own liberation (Life Cycle: 6. Liberation) and as a genuine company community (Life Cycle: 7. Community) became market leaders in their branch of trade. The chief carefully monitored the process of giving trust, sharing the truth, respect, daring, humanity and dignity. At the same time he kept an eye on the whole picture (Life Cycle: 8. Embracing) so as to be prepared for the unexpected because he knew there would always be new cycles –new endings and beginnings. (Life Cycle: 9.Full Ending).

Collective Summary Note

A COLLECTIVE is premised in practice on motivation, cooperation, and communication. It is about achieving the best possible result to the benefit of the entire collective; IDENTITY that has MEANING, made manifest. The balanced collective opens the space for something new, unique, and not expected—the realm of wellbeing for all. There is a "KINGDOM" in harmony.

7- Community
  Eternity - Manifest
	8- Embracement
	  Foundation - We
	
		9- Full ending
		  Kingdom - Abundance

'This we know; all things are connected, like the blood that unites us. We do not weave the web of life; we are merely a strand in it. Whatever we do to the web, we do to ourselves'. Chief Seattle	"Yesterday I was clever, so I wanted to change the world. Today I am wise, so I am changing myself'
	                    Muhammad Rumi
		'Without forgiveness life is governed by an endless cycle of resentment and retaliation'
		                    Roberto Assagioli.

What the ULC brings is methodology through a Trinity matrix structure and the use of art to guide people through awareness, dialogue and forgiveness on the road to achieving a life of fulfillment and harmony. At the full ending, a new cycle starts at a higher state of awareness:

NOT EXPECTED ∞ FULL ENDING ∞ NOT EXPECTED

∞

12 NOT EXPECTED-Trinity of leadership

A new thought-emerged: - Trinity of leadership
                                 - Profiling Soul and Inner Knowing so called soft aspects

> *"When I examine myself and my methods of thought, I come close to the conclusion that the gift of imagination has meant more to me than any talent for absorbing absolute knowledge … All great achievements of science must start from intuitive knowledge. I believe in intuition and inspiration … At times I feel certain I am right while not knowing the reason"* (edited by Paul Schilpp, 1979, Albert Einstein: Autobiographical Notes).

How often in life, when faced with a challenge as an individual, do we not have the courage to voice our opinion? The ULC helps us to know ourselves better and so find the confidence to voice our point of view.

The trinity concept is an intriguing model. I am talking here about the Rainmaker, the Hunter, and the Messenger. Each of the three represents a particular energy that manifests in particular talents, abilities, actions, and ways of being and doing.

The trinity concept is a unity of three leaders at the top of the organization structure. They respectfully, openly, and readily engage in dialogue with those who are voicing their fears, encouraging their hopes and the wisdom required for activating higher levels of consciousness. In this context, dialogue is a process that has emerged from the necessity of the times we live in, but it is not yet embedded in our culture. This is a social skill that seeks to heal the imbalances of the past in a matter-driven society. The lekgotla, an encounter in dialogue, is an indigenous process that resides deep in the hearts and minds of people. (My first book in 2002: *Lekgotla: The Art of Leadership through Dialogue*).

Rainmaker—Hunter—Messenger concept

Trinity of leaders	Rainmaker/spirit Envisioning I am that I am	Hunter/ mind-thinking Rational doing I am therefore I think	Messenger/heart-feeling Embracing I am because we are

"Happiness is when what you think [hunter], what you say [messenger], and what you do are in harmony [rainmaker]." Mahatma Gandhi

This quote by Gandhi captures the idea of balance well. A united trinity of leaders can protect against the potentially inflated ego of a single leader. If these leaders work as one, society will flourish. In larger organizations and in society, each role in the trinity is normally fulfilled by a number of different people (executive teams, boards). In smaller organizations, however, it is likely that one person may combine two or more of these roles. The following trinity roles of interdependent leadership are important for building effective organizations.

The Rainmaker
The energy of the rainmaker emanates from thought.

- The Rainmaker energy has the ability to share thought (vision, concept, ideas) that speak to both the hearts and minds of people. The Rainmaker's ideas can shift communities, societies, countries, and the world.
- The Rainmaker energy plays an important role at every phase of the ULC, providing Thought, Vision and Feeling, binding and inspiring the Collective.
- The Rainmaker is the creative spark. He speaks to the imagination. Without a vision, people remain focused on what is and not what could be.

The Hunter
The energy of the Hunter emanates from the mind.

Although the vision of the Rainmaker is significant in building a collective/organization, the role of the Hunter is critical to the successful implementation of that vision. The Hunter addresses the root cause of problems and creates breakthrough.

- The Hunter is the executive who realizes the vision in a tangible way so that the vision is implemented through action.
- The effort of the Hunter is aligned to the vision of the Rainmaker.
- To sustain the vision, both the Rainmaker and the Hunter need the support of the Messenger to keep the vision alive in the collective.

The Messenger
The energy of the Messenger emanates from the heart.

The Messenger facilitates the organization/society feeling as one. Each member being a part of the shared knowing and shared consciousness that is the basis of all individual and collective action.

Without the connecting energy of the Messenger, the whole would become fragmented (silos).

- The Messenger energy works with intuition, emotion, and communication. The Messenger is the moral compass, holding up the mirror to the collective. They always speak the truth, create alignment between thinking and feeling, and ensure that any action taken is in the best interest of the collective.
- The Messenger plays an important role as the facilitator of communication and dialogue as well as being the guardian of the wellbeing of the collective (feeling).
- The Messengers are the poets that capture and express the feelings of the collective without passing judgment. They help gauge and facilitate the health of the collective.

All three of these energies are needed to ensure a healthy, harmonious, sustainable collective (relationships, family, community, society, companies, countries, etc.). Each of these energies is needed to unlock and nurture the natural leadership potential of every individual in the collective. These three stereotypes are driven from their inner knowing (the finger print of their soul).

Let's walk through the life cycle with the Rainmaker, Hunter and Messenger.

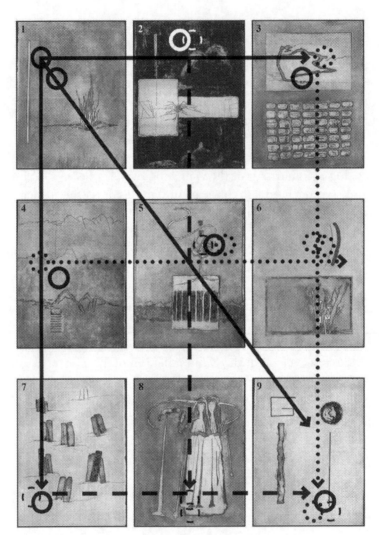

Leadership matrix

ULC Trinity Leadership Matrix

I. Identity	1 Not expected **R/ R**	2 Encounter **H/ R**	3 Transformation **M/ R**
II. Meaning	4 Movement **R/ M**	5 Enlightenment **H/ M/ R**	6 Liberation **M/ M**
III. Collective	7 Community **R/ H**	8 Embracement **H/ H**	9 Full ending **H/ M/ R**

R = Rainmaker Thought (vertical) - Identity (horizontal) and Thought (diagonally)
H = Hunter Senses (vertical) and Collective (horizontal)
M = Messenger Awareness (vertical) and Meaning (horizontal)

Charlene Smith, in her book Committed to Me, writes:

> *The world and history abound with men and women who appeared to be good until they attained power, but once in positions of influence became despotic, intolerant, angry, and vengeful and generally people history now despises. What made them undergo such apparently profound personality changes?*

The ULC might help to understand why Charlene's observations still happen again and again.

If we have one dominating leader:

- Rainmaker 1- R/R can become stuck in his thought, risk a dreamer as creative thinker. Vision without action

- Hunter 8-H/H can become an authoritarian leader under the umbrella of a company or government or church leader misusing the philosophy/vision for his own interest. Action without a vision

- Messenger 6-M/M can become a dogmatic [socialism /communism/capitalism or religious fanatic] leader.
  Action without unconditional love

Soloist leaders

As a result, the society will be out of balance. This is to-day's reality on earth.

The ULC is a simple tool, practical for a diagnosis of which leadership style of an organization, community or country is needed, in which circumstances.

If the Not expected happens: Visionary leader, R/R or H/R, supported by a strong Hunter and Messenger is required. If you have a charismatic Hunter, H/H, then it is extremely important that balance comes in. This leader has to listen to his Rainmaker and Messenger or, using the model of situational leadership, empower the Rainmaker/Messenger to carry out the process of restoring meaning in the community or organization. To apply this thought, learn to practice with the trinity of leadership, propose this structure to the collective. It is exposing oneself to the collective.

Activities to build peace by nurturing visionary leadership, strengthens personal responsibility and so manifests the vision held by inspired people. May I invite you to use your own imagination, inspiration and courage to use these model suggestions in practice?

Leadership trinity

Polarity opponents united as oneness: Give it a thought; the trinity of leaders.

PHASE 1

X needs a new vision/thought of a Rainmaker to avoid arrogance or stagnation in sustainability.
B needs a Hunter to create a breakthrough, implementing the thought of the Rainmaker

PHASE 2
Needs a new leadership style

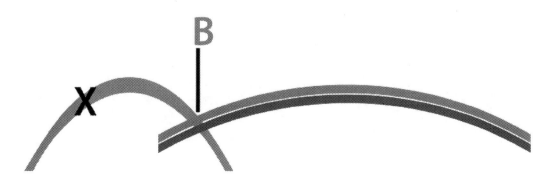

B Hunter hands over to a Messenger/Rainmaker, stabilizing to create sustainability. After a period of time the Rainmaker Hunter starts new thoughts/creative thinking, preparing for change [continuous change is the only stable factor in the universe]. The Messenger is preparing for letting go of the past to create space in the mind, to be open and accepting the new vision.

The ULC provides a guide to find the individual's talents, how they can support one another.

Leadership Wheel: the Hunter in the driver's seat, then the Messenger then the Rainmaker but, important from an internal/external view, they are perceived as one. Embrace the uncommon leadership thinking of unconditional love, giving energy to all there is.

In our hectic daily lives, listening to the echo of the ego, we have forgotten to realize the vision of working in harmony, giving of our best within the collective, to achieve higher levels of peace and prosperity. It is not about promoting a political doctrine, not at all. It is creating metaphors, awareness and the ULC roadmap to life in harmony, and creating prosperity. All the ingredients are at hand if we wish to see feel and manifest our thoughts at a higher individual and collective conscious awareness level.

People with a high level of fear for their existence have a lot of stress, becoming uncertain as to how to handle change. Whereas people with a low level of fear are well positioned to handle uncertainty, stress and change. The uncertain people see the others, who view change and uncertainty as an opportunity to create new forms for sustainability, as the architects of the developing society. This in fact, compounds the problem for the uncertain people to remember who they really are, what their role is. This empty feeling is the playground for the echo of the ego 'telling you that you need certainty' while in reality you become more insecure. If you know who you are, you become the master with the talents you have, and you shift your fear in a positive emotional behavior towards the journey through life. You are inspiring people through embracing leadership.

If we know who we are we can support and create organizations and a society that works for all of us.

Which energy when?

The question people often ask when do I need the Rainmaker, Hunter or Messenger?

> Relative to the ULC Trinity Leadership matrix, if an organization has a problem with the judgment of an issue in "5 - the Enlightenment" intersection, we need Rainmaker, Hunter and Messenger energy, with strong input from the Rainmaker for a thought to solve the disagreement or duality; left and right cadres - the Not Expected.

> When we look at "8 - the Embracement" intersection we can imagine that, with the dominant Hunter/ Hunter , it could happen that in the right and left cadres, the encounter - Rainmaker and Hunter, the Rainmaker is overpowered by the Hunter, with all the consequences for the organization.

In the table below you will find which skills are needed when. Profiling of the managers, or a small team, gives objective information as to why there is disagreement and which skills are missing.

ROADMAP INDICATOR FOR WHICH TRINITY
OF LEADERSHIP ENERGY IS NEEDED WHEN
&
The process of awareness-reconciliation-forgiveness

The behavioral aspects for each Intersection in Phase one IDENTITY below are summarized in: Chapter 7: Phase 1: Identity roadmap for transformation and change.

The behavioral aspects for each Intersection in Phase two MEANING below are summarized in: Chapter 10: Phase II: Meaning roadmap for transformation and letting go of the past.

The behavioral aspects for each Intersection in Phase three COLLECTIVE below are summarized in: Chapter 11: Phase III: Collective roadmap for prosperity and sustainability.

The thinking mind A Manifest	Source: energy of infinity ∞ Envisioning	Feeling heart B Unconditional love
⇌	Phase one IDENTITY ⇌	
Enlightenment R/H/M Judgment *How can an event or thought be ex explained? Analysis of multiple Perceptions.*	1-Not expected R/R Thought & Wisdom *Rainmaker called for envisioning. A call for action*	Enlightenment R/H/M Reconciliation *How does the event or the thought touch people's hearts? (Emotional effect)*
Movement R/M Mercy *What is it that the people tell us? Analysis of multiple perceptions. Down to earth solutions*	2-Encounter H/R Senses & Understanding *Open dialogue!* Sharing the truth	Movement R/M Feeling *How do people feel in the current situation? Understanding of emotional dissatisfaction.*
Embracement H/H Foundation *Practical and content wise preparation for change. Learning HOW.*	3-Transformation M/R Awareness & Knowledge *Being united* Setting the goals	Embracement H/H We *Keep in touch/supporting people's confidence (reducing fear and uncertainty concerning an upcoming change)*
⇌	Phase two MEANING ⇌	
Liberation M/M Beauty (form) *How am I going to add value to the change? Result setting.*	4-Movement R/M Feeling & Mercy Coming into action	Liberation M/M Forgiveness *Trusting the change. Conviction in the way we go.*
Not expected R/R Wisdom *Just do it. The logical go through of the planned route.*	5-Enlightenment R/H/M Reconciliation & Judgment *Collective vision* Letting go the past	Not expected R/R Thought *Personal growth. The things I learn and the goals I reach.*
Transformation M/R Knowledge *The adding value of my talents. Pro-active implementation of the strategy.*	6-Liberation M/M Forgiveness & Beauty Passion and purpose	Transformation M/R Awareness *Yes, we can. Enjoyment of the positive atmosphere.*

The thinking mind A Manifest	Source: energy of infinity ∞ Envisioning	Feeling heart B Unconditional love
⇔ **Phase three COLLECTIVE** ⇔		
Community R/ H Eternity *Power of the collective. 1+1 = 3.*	7-Community R/ H Manifest & Eternity Purpose and vision aligned	Community R/ H Manifest *We are family. We know who we are.*
Encounter H/R Understanding *Stay alert. Critical measuring of results and improving within the ongoing strategy.*	8-Embracement H/H We & Foundation Either keep on going sensitively or becoming arrogant	Encounter H/R Senses *Living the conviction. Definitively overcoming the fear for the future and avoiding the power of dominance.*
Full ending R/H/M Kingdom *Improving till perfection. Internal auditing and critical attitude towards possible improvements.*	9-Full ending R/H/M Abundance & Kingdom Emerge of the next vision	Full ending R/H/M Abundance *This is the future. Forgiveness of the past. The power of NOW.*

Story 21: Trinity of leadership in action.

Story: Enlightenment a realistic judgment of the market situation.
Actions: **Not expected R/R and Enlightenment R/H/M and Not expected R/R**

What stays standing after a cold and rainy night? A 'We' organization, that produces building insulation products, has a market share of thirty percent. Its main competitor had fifty five percent of the market and other, smaller players in the industry hold the rest. The market is characterized by stiff price competition and the customers, whose decisions are driven solely by price, have no loyalty to any particular brand despite some compelling features in the 'We' organization's products, such as improved water resistance. The company decides to engage in a series of dialogues with its distributors about this added value. Following these dialogues, the company begins to offer product education to its distributors and organizes a series of contact meetings between the distributors and the architects.

The company offers its distributors support in marketing its products and, further, offers them a price structure based on the volumes they purchase. The A class of distributors receives a discount of 40% the B class 30 % and the C class 20%. During these meetings, some of the distributors become upset because of the fixed pricing structure.

Out of the Lekgotla's held with the nearly four hundred distributors, the company convinces only seventy of the attending distributors, of the value of trust and sharing market knowledge between all the parties, as well as of going to the end-users as one united entity. At the same time, the company launched a quality campaign at the building sites. Production employees drove female employees around the country, showing the bricklayers how to use the products, using the slogan: 'What stays standing after a cold and rainy night?' The outcome was that the users appreciated the extra lengths that the producers went through to make them feel a part of the company and developed a strong preference for this We organization's products. The bricklayers also found the 'We' organization's product easier to use after the training they had received. The end architects, dealers and producer were united. This is the power of embracing the 'We'.

One year later the 'We' organization had increased its market share from 30 % to 52%, because it engaged its customers in dialogue, meaning and improved its added value offering. Its customers have begun to view a low price as being less important than quality and service.

The Different and Complementary Roles of the Trinity

Role of Rainmaker Energy

Horizontal—The not expected results in the thought (Rainmaker/Rainmaker); the vision, followed by an encounter, translates into the formation of a practical identity in the individual/collective (Rainmaker/Hunter); this results in a transformation that creates awareness in the collective (Rainmaker/Messenger).

Vertical—At the same time, the thought must spark a feeling if the vision is to become manifest and meaningful for a collective.

Diagonally— The energy of the rainmaker is important to expose at the Enlightenment, especially his energy of unconditional love, needed in the process of reconciliation. Examples of such leaders were Gandhi and Mandela.

We can see that the major contribution of the Rainmaker's energy is to present the thought, which creates the environment for the Not expected. The Rainmaker energy is overlapping here. A double energy in the Not expected can cause unrealistic thoughts. The vision is that spark from which everything follows. However the Rainmaker is also a sort of guide or compass through the process. The Rainmaker is the beginning and the end of the circle of infinity. In the Trinity of Leadership model, the Rainmaker needs the support of the Hunter and Messenger, and they in turn have this interdependence for realizing the vision, resulting in sustainable tangible results.

Role of Hunter Energy

Horizontal—The community, formed around the vision, must manifest practically if there is to be any action (Rainmaker/Hunter). This physical state must become embracement, the individual in the collective and the collective in the individual, if a strong collective (Hunter/Hunter) is to be formed, where individuals act on the vision to the best of their unique and personal abilities. When this occurs, it creates space for practical forgiveness (Hunter/Messenger), the higher state of letting go in trust and harmony.

Vertical—A tangible identity is formed by the individual/collective (Rainmaker/Hunter) around the vision, which becomes tangibly meaningful. If needed reconciliation can take place, the energy flow of Enlightenment. (Hunter/Messenger/Rainmaker) The effect is that the collective is bonded. (Hunter/Hunter). (Collective here is unity, in diversity, in action).

We can see that the major contribution of the Hunter's energy is to the collective: there must be embracement of the vision, practically; at the level of the individual (internal) and collective (external) if it is to be realized. The Hunter energy is overlapping here at the embracement; this is a phase were the Hunter can become the dominant power. This is the foundation phase whereby the vision is able to move through its full cycle toward the creation of a new reality.

Role of Messenger Energy

Horizontal—There is movement in the individual/collective, which creates a feeling that the vision is right (Rainmaker/Messenger), but this needs reconciliation—enlightenment—in order to become meaning, to have purpose. This process is cemented by liberation, freedom from conditioning, negative beliefs, old patterns of behavior, and blockages, which results in forgiveness with the past and peace.

Vertical—The awareness in identity is important for the soul of the individual/collective (Rainmaker/Messenger) if there is to be forgiveness with the past (Messenger/Messenger), without which the individual/collective cannot achieve forgiveness (Hunter/Messenger/Rainmaker) (sustainable forgiveness), and here is the ending of one cycle, the ritual burning of the past toward a new beginning.

We can see that the major contribution of the Messenger's energy is to help with forgiveness, so that there is liberation from the past; the Messenger energy is overlapping here at the liberation, a risk of dogmatic beliefs overpowering the individuals. This is a breaking of the prison of the past that allows the individual/collective to come into unity in action.

Note: Moving through the source matrix, we can see how important the Rainmaker energy is in providing the spark and guidance for the Hunter and Messenger energies. It must hold the vision, but it cannot execute it by itself. The Hunter and Messenger, the "I" and the "We," need to come into balance, in harmony, to create the full ending and complete the cycle: opening the gateway to new, inspiring thoughts, which result in sustainability—a flood of energy in imagination, creativity, innovation, and well-being, driven for and by the individual for the collective. This trinity carries the same importance as Identity, Meaning and Collective. In fact, it is an integral part of it. None is more important than the other, and alone, unique talents and abilities are not enough to have the vision realized. What is needed is thought, manifesting, passionate leadership, burning the past, creating purpose and where the people carry the vision.

Burn the past

124

Moving through Each Phase of the ULC Matrix

<u>Identity</u>

1. Not expected
   Thought: This is pure Rainmaker energy. It is a unique, visionary energy that arrives unexpectedly in the mind and heart. Its impact is always profound. There is wisdom and the quality of being wise in the thought. It opens the window to a new reality that speaks to the mind and the heart of people.

   Note: Dual Rainmaker energies here can lead to a vision lacking the ability for meaning and action—utopian. There is imbalance in the Rainmaker's energy.

2. Encounter
   Senses: This is mixed Rainmaker-Hunter energy. In this phase, there is a physical coming together in dialogue with the intention of forming an identity around the vision. The Rainmaker's role here is to hold the space for the vision while the Hunter executes it practically. The Hunter has a keen intuitive awareness or feeling to the presence of importance of the thought. He, the Hunter, senses an external stimulus that enables him to come in action. He uses his power and talent so that the individuals have the ability to understand the thought.

   Note: If the identity is weak or does not resonate in the hearts of the collective, then there is the potential for the hunter, through arrogance, to become the dominant energy at the expense of either the vision or the collective or both. If there is no understanding, there is imbalance between the individuals.

3. Transformation
   Awareness: This is mixed Rainmaker-Messenger energy. At this phase, the vision, through tangible awareness, manifests itself as collective awareness; the inward knowing begins to be expressed outwardly by individuals and collectives. It is the invisible radiation of energy, the setting of the phase for meaning. The completion of identity is putting the cement between the bricks. It is the philosophy or belief in action, the skill in service for the whole. The soul unfolds itself, like a lotus with countless petals.

   Note: If the Rainmaker is unable to properly convey the vision, then the identity that is created is fragile or lacking in substance. At the same time, if the messenger becomes dominant, there is a risk that the substance of the vision will be lost in pontification and dogma. Possible first barrier as in Story 5: Miracle of Life.

Summary Identity: In this phase, the Rainmaker, Hunter, and Messenger need to come into alignment through trinity in a way that the vision takes form in matter and spirit toward the creation of Meaning. If there is a blockage, this phase can result in an identity that is lacking substance or is imposed or dogmatic.

Meaning

4. Movement
   Feeling: This is mixed Rainmaker-Messenger energy. Here the Messenger is an important advisor in the way that he can bridge truth and understanding. The vision becomes a strong feeling in the individual and collective. From a basis of awareness, this is a foundational phase of meaning making, where belief inspires action. This continuation of the internal process becomes externally tangible. People want to perform out of desire, motivated by compassion and mercy.

   Note: If the Rainmaker is unable to translate the thought into feeling, then it will lack the ability to become meaningful. In reverse, if the Messenger is not inline, then there will be no gravity or truth in what is spoken about the vision. There is no mercy.

5. Enlightenment
   Reconciliation: This is mixed Hunter-Messenger energy. The Hunter guides the Messenger through action while the Messenger reflects if this is in the best interest of the community. Is there a feeling of reconciliation? At this phase, individual and collective enlightenment lead to a decision around acceptance of the vision. The Hunter guides the Messenger through action while the Messenger reflects if this is in the best interest. There is the feeling of judgment without prejudice.

   Note: If the Hunter energy is dominant, then the mind becomes the controlling force, with the result that any action is lacking in heart (feeling). When the messenger is overpowering, then any action is limited by strong beliefs that can overpower the vision's desire to be realized. The impact in both situations is ruled by duality where reconciliation taking place in reality is mostly impossible. The Echo of the ego .The enlightenment phase is often the stumbling block of individuals and collectives as they are unable to find the balance needed to create space for reconciliation. Possible second barrier

6. Liberation
   Forgiveness: This is full Messenger energy. In this phase, Messenger guides the individual or the collective in the process of making peace with the past, letting go of conditioning patterns, and managing fear. The inspiring energy of meaning is needed

for forgiveness. If there is liberation, then the energy flows freely into the community. There is beauty that pleases the society's knowing and moral senses. The barriers of the conditioners of our thinking are passed. There is the beauty of trust.

Note: There is a risk of the Messenger becoming dominant here if his dogmatic ideas are over powering people. From this position, meaning can develop duality through dogmas and beliefs, which are not universally beneficial for the individual or collective. There is no beauty, no real forgiveness. Possible third barrier

Summary Meaning: In this phase, the Rainmaker, Hunter, and Messenger need to come into alignment (synchronicity) through trinity in a way that the vision becomes meaningful for the Collective. Reconciliation and forgiveness are practiced in daily life.

Collective

7. Community
   Manifest: This is mixed Rainmaker-Hunter energy. Community is the beginning of the vision becoming form in matter. This is the individual and collective in balance toward manifesting the thought through action. The wellbeing of the collective is also important here as it provides the guiding and creating energies needed for the cycle to come to completion. This is a crucial phase in which the vision needs to have content in reality—down-to-earth. The identity has meaning, and the people carry the vision. There is eternity; the dam is full of positive energy, and the floodgates are being opened.

8. Embracement
   We: This is full Hunter energy. The forming of a strong collective is key if the cycle is to complete itself. The individual or collective is committed to add its unique talents to the benefit of all. There is unity in diversity as different voices sing together in harmony to create a unified hymn; the many parts that make up a whole embrace the vision, own it, and drive it: A sustainable foundation. Be aware that the ego energy can lead to the dominance of "we are the strongest," "we are the best."

   Note: *There is a risk here that the double Hunter energy is out of balance, creating space for arrogance and dominance of the few over the many. If there is an imbalance through dogmas, arrogance, false beliefs, or complacency in the face of success, it can undo the entire process. Possible fourth barrier*

9. Full Ending
   Abundance: This is mixed Hunter-Messenger energy. This is the completion of the cycle as the energy of the individual or collective moves from one phase to another. The

energy flow, through polarity, results in the birth of matter and spirit in harmony. The balanced collective opens the space for something new, unique, and not expected—the realm of wellbeing for all. There is a "KINGDOM" in harmony.

Summary Collective: In this phase, the Rainmaker, Hunter, and Messenger, the Trinity, through polarity, open the gateway to new, inspiring thoughts that result in sustainability: a flood of energy in imagination, creativity, and well-being emerge.

Embracing Leadership

If leaders have the courage to expose themselves to the collective, they will be surprised at the positive outcome—the Not expected. The ULC navigator helps individuals and the collective to become aware of the path to follow: a path of polarity, where we tap into the infinite wisdom of humanity. On this path we combine the thinking and the feeling with our awareness of the soul's inner knowing, wherein we understand where the blockages are and what to do to go through the barriers in the difficult process of awareness, reconciliation, forgiveness, and embracing the ego, all of which are needed in times of change.

These steps are necessary to make transformation in organizations sustainable. It is a dance between the 'I' and the 'We'. It represents the 'I' embracing the 'We' and the 'We' embracing the 'I'.

Linear thinking process

In this linear process we follow the path from the not expected (1), straight to movement (4), into action: cost reduction, we need better communication, entrepreneurship of the employees and so on. Following this rhetoric the road map of the reorganization is presented as the 'transformation" strategy to the people by the thinking and knowing elite. We need more inspired and passionate people, is the rhetoric of management. There is no change in behavior; it still is them and us.

The linear event/thinking process has difficulty in passing the barrier of transformation and moving into the meaning phase. To pass the hurdles of reconciliation and forgiveness is almost impossible in an analytical thinking model.

What is needed here are the soft human aspects. Individuals and society must become aware that we have to liberate ourselves from our stigmatizing dogmas and false beliefs, listening to our ego advisor, playing the victim of the selfish and not accessing our inner knowing. This can be achieved by going in depth, through the process of awareness, to activate the wisdom of the crowd. Lekgotla, an encounter with all members of the organization/community, is an answer.

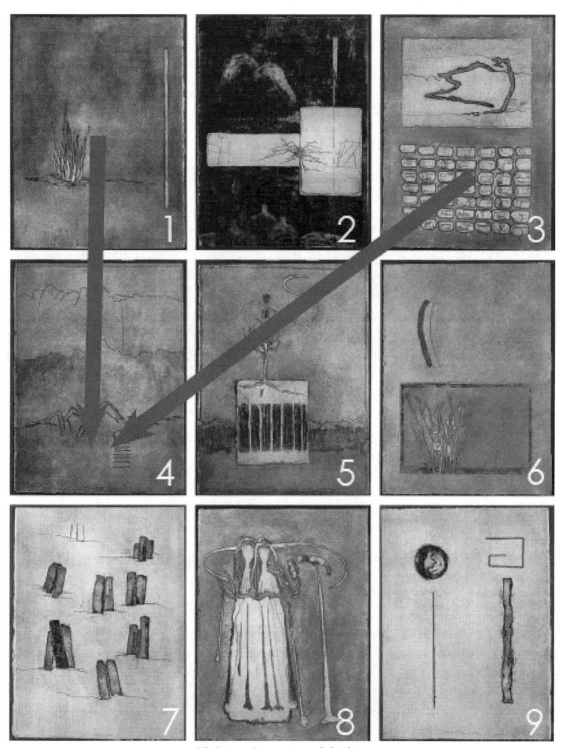

ULC steps-Event oriented thinking

The ULC as a Guide

How often in life, when faced with a challenge as an Individual/Collective, does our thirst for a solution turn outward? And in the process of looking to the world we find many examples. We see the wisdom in their answers. But these do not seem to fit with that situation we are facing and so a solution is illusive.

Yes, these examples can act as yardsticks, but can they ever completely or adequately tackle the problem as a "cut and paste" solution? The answers to Individual/Collective challenge must come from within. Think of how consultants, advisors, psychologists and so on, often just get us to a point of understanding, maybe through clever concepts or with words, which only confirmed what we already knew? The source of and solution to any problem is always within.

In this sense, the ULC is one such guide in working through cycles. Does the ULC provide the answers? Yes. Can the ULC solve the issues? No. Only people, the members of an organization/community are, as members of the collective, a natural part of the problem. An attitude of willingness can solve the issues through dialogue and really listening to the other person. But the ULC may help to frame the questions, to identify the blockages and areas needing focused attention. It may help facilitate the process of moving through a cycle by providing a conceptual framework, and it might even come to act as a reference tool to monitor future cycles. The ULC may do all of this, but it remains, crucially, universal. Its universal nature is only meant as a tool to help facilitate the unlocking of (Individual/Collective) internal wisdom, to point out what is already there.

Working in this way, we have seen the potential of the ULC to empower people by making them see that they have everything they need to change their situation. If the approach was only rational the ULC would simply not function, that is against the ULC's spirit/energy and against the infinite wisdom within each of us.

The sustainability of organizations /communities is developed through understanding the following universal leadership principles:

- All of us are a part of the whole.
- Leaders/managers know themselves and their capabilities intimately.
- Leaders/managers expose their true selves to the collective.

The following characteristics epitomize "We" organizations/communities, which operate under Embracing Leadership philosophy:

- Members have an improved awareness of what has to be done as a result of the open dialogues in which they have been participating and have exposed themselves.
- People work in harmony together as a result of engaging in these dialogues, which have paved the way for awareness, reconciliation and forgiveness.
- Individuals have a choice to participate honestly in the Embracing Leadership style organization.

We live at a time of a unique opportunity to explore the evolution of letting go of the echo of the ego.

Stuck in fear and dominance

WE embracing the I

Flow of spiritual energy

The choice is yours

Without it society will be out of balance. This is to-day's reality on earth. The ULC is a simple tool, practical for a diagnosis of which leadership style of an organization, community or country is needed, in which circumstances.

Story 22: A Branch of Imbalance

A subsidiary of a large IT company was having problems at the level of senior management. This situation was seriously hurting business. The inherited complex matrix structure was a key factor contributing to the existence of silos within the business, something that had resulted in a frustrated leadership who retreated into the trenches and fought one another with the weapons of pointed fingers and blame.

At the same time, the company was undergoing a global restructuring process, which was only adding fuel to the fire. This process was being poorly communicated, and senior staff felt uncertain, confused, and suspicious. Some were even looking for other opportunities outside the business. The different departments were like oxen harnessed to a beautiful wagon, but each was trying to pull in its own direction.

The CEO was a decent man who had softer talents for working with people. He was wise, trustworthy, forward thinking, and able to create an environment of harmony. His ability to reflect on things also meant that he was a good foundation for the business. However, the tendency to be slow in making decisions was hurting him and alienating his team.

Individual interviews were set up with the extended executive board as a means to get to the root of the problem. Each person was first asked to select an image from the ULC that reflected the company's problems for them at that moment in time. What quickly, and clearly, emerged was that the company had no real identity, the result being that the people had no deeper sense of meaning. The result was a broken collective.

The process of creating the profiles revealed that this was a dynamic, highly skilled collective made up of individuals who were driven to make the company succeed. Many of them were quick to explain what they thought were the causes, as well as offer, in most cases, strong potential solutions. So what was the problem?

Something that became clear was that many of these individuals had been put into positions or made responsible for aspects of the business that were not aligned to their particular talents and abilities. For example, one team member was being moved from a more finance-focused position to one where the person would be managing people. The concern of this person was that he or she did not know how to get the team to work together. Another individual had a long history in sales and customer engagement, having served for many years in the company.

The concern of this person was that they were under pressure to meet increasingly demanding sales targets when their true talent was nurturing the customer.

"I don't sell products, I sell solutions," was the comment of the after sales director, "And people don't buy products, they buy people." The frustration of this director was that his attention was being shifted away from nurturing clients toward chasing numbers and performing administrative tasks. How, then, could this company effectively realign? How could he turn the ship around?

Taking the overall picture that came from the selections, as well as the individual profiles, it was possible to reorganize the existing picture into one where the mix of talents was better aligned.

Starting with the CEO in the center, as the chief, my proposed structure was arranged in a circular rather than hierarchical fashion. Individuals were split up into smaller collectives where their particular talents could be best utilized. There were those who were more left-brained and whose contribution would be better felt if they were allowed to perform the more rational, process-orientated, administrative functions. Two collectives were envisaged here: operations managers and analytical managers.

On the other side were those who were more right-brained and whose contributions would be better felt if they were allowed to perform the more emotional, creative, and people-oriented functions. Two collectives were envisaged here: creative leaders and service rendering. A diagram was created of these talents so that the proposed structure was made visible.

Think of any collective and how the different, but complementary, functions are needed to create harmony and prosperity. There are those who take risks and bring in ideas (rainmakers), those who pave the way and execute the vision (hunters), and then others who hold everything together, performing maintenance from behind (messengers).

It was interesting to see how the company's initial picture was unbalanced, whereby individuals were being expected to perform tasks that did not fit with their talents. When rational people are pushed into more emotional roles, or vice versa, they are likely to feel out of their depth. This is very often the case and is a great source of frustration and even stress as people are asked to be something they are not. Imagine an accountant being asked to head up a sales team—or a creative director being told he or she must manage a company audit?

The tendency in such a situation is for a collective to look outside for solutions or to begin to sacrifice some of its parts. The divide-and-rule mentality generally rears its ugly head when a collective is broken, and individuals, now frustrated, become focused on self-interest. Individuals and collectives thrive and prosper when there is harmony, when talents are acknowledged and embraced, when people are able to give their best to the collective, and when the journey is not made more important than the destination.

By analyzing the state of the collective and the individual, it is possible to see where the blockages and misalignments are. From here, an honest dialogue can create a foundation for trust. Through this, agreement comes as to the way forward, inspiration and motivation—the sparks of individual and collective action. The problem and solution can come from the same source. If there is receptiveness to the process, then the individual can benefit from a strong sense of identity, meaning, and collective, while the collective can navigate the road of awareness, reconciliation, and forgiveness. This twin path, when in balance, is supported by thought that creates feeling that makes manifest. Inside of this, the collective is able to unlock the wisdom of the individual while the individual contributes to the health and longevity of the collective. This is an example of the individual-collective map created for the company.

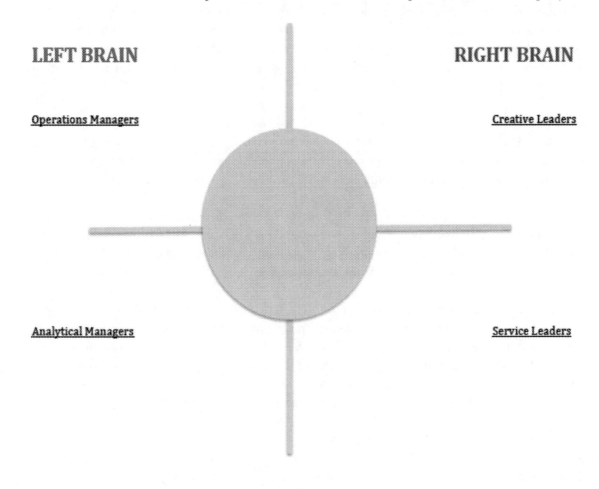

LEFT BRAIN

RIGHT BRAIN

Operations Managers

Creative Leaders

Analytical Managers

Service Leaders

The Individual or Collective in Balance

So what does an individual or collective in balance look like?

There are many answers to this question, maybe even an infinite number, for the detail of every picture is different. The not expected happens; a new thought comes from the rainmaker energy. The left side, the "I," the hunter energy, inside of enlightenment, must engage it. At the same time, it must be engaged by the right side, the "we," the messenger energy, inside of enlightenment.

If these two become one in polarity and find balance, then meaning is the result. When a vision or idea—thought—strikes a chord of meaning, then wisdom results. This is the fruit of the completed stage that is carried forward to the next one. If the cycle is navigated inside a relationship of balance, then the flow is seamless.

Practically speaking, every manifestation of this will be different. The picture will be as diverse as the elements it is composed of. However, what we can say of this is that the picture, when in balance, will be one of harmony, communication, cooperation, prosperity, and sustainability over the long term is the end result.

The Importance of Trinity a Not Expected Thought

> May I invite you as leader to have an encounter with your crewmembers over polarity versus duality and the power of trinity?
>
> The invitation is the Not expected, where you as an embracing leader expose yourself to the employees.

Note: A strange act of self-denial, created Duality.
Polarity is the energy of harmony in contrast, and therefore Unity. Duality is the energy of disconnection. Human beings have made a significant departure from being in balance with the universe. The more we have divided, the further we have separated from our true self. Duality became the source of our imbalance.

Emotionally, mentally, physically, politically, economically, socially, environmentally, we find imbalance by enslaving ourselves to the relentless/endless pursuit to produce economic growth. The biggest challenge for the world is to bring purpose and stabilization back in our lives. We have to dig to the bottom of why human nature causes so many conflicts and chaos. Before Babel we could settle conflicts through dialogue, dialogue was the highest form of war. Moving from hunter-gatherers, after farming was introduced, to hunter-worriers, the story of Babel.

If we know who we are, we can support and create organizations and a society that works for all of us. Awaken the universe within.

Historical examples of visionary leaders – vision in action, leaders uncommon in their thinking. In companies we see the same patterns by visionary leaders like Bill Gates, the late Steve Jobs and so on.

Question to reflect on:

- If we have great leaders why are we not able to create a better world?
- Might the answer be a consciousness leapfrogging propelling innovations in leadership?

Winston Churchill vision speech Aug 1949
"There is no reason for us not to succeed in achieving our goal and laying the foundation of a United Europe. A Europe whose moral design will win the respect and acknowledgement of all humanity, and whose physical strength will be such that no person will dare to disturb it as it marches peacefully towards the future."

Mandela's vision: A Rainbow nation- Equality- Reconciliation

Mr. George Bizos - Mandela's old friend was speaking at a celebration and memorial for Mandela at the University of the Witwatersrand in Johannesburg: He said "Mandela had a vision of a country that was to be free of poverty and corruption, and never wanted the country to be a "one man" state."

The wisdom of Gandhi is expressed in his search for truth, his insistence upon *Ahimsa* 'non-violence'. Barack Obama's address at Nelson Mandela's memorial service [A sentence, December 2013] in which Obama touched people's hearts, around the world: "The questions we face today – how to promote equality and justice; to uphold freedom and human rights; to end conflict and sectarian war – do not have easy answers. But there were no easy answers in front of that child in Qunu. Nelson Mandela reminds us that it always seems impossible until it is done. South Africa shows us, that is true. South Africa shows us we can change. We can choose to live in a world defined not by our differences, but by our common hopes. We can choose a world defined not by conflict, but by peace and justice and opportunity" Why are we not contributing to these thoughts/visions saying: Yes we can, let's start small at our workplace/ communities we life or just yourself and the family. In the physical world, our experience, our perception, is material and so this is what we take as real. Our physical experience of the world is through our senses, so, in the process of sensing the world it is easy to lose touch with those invisible, intangible things in and around us. Sensory experience creates the perception that the world of matter is all that there is and so Matter Consciousness, through Thinking and Knowing, has become dominant in us. The result has been a disconnection with our Spirit Consciousness and therefore the wholeness of our being.

Marshall's vision changes the world. It renewed Europe's identity, giving people meaning and binding the collective to work together. By the spring of 1945, the Germans had surrendered and Europe was liberated. Marshall was then appointed Secretary of State in January 1947. The European economy was still in ruins; there was great political instability and widespread personal suffering as a result of the war. At a conference of foreign ministers in Russia shortly thereafter, Marshall spoke with Joseph Stalin about working with the United States to provide aid to ruined Europe. Stalin was not interested. Marshall came to realize that the United States would be on its own in its attempts to help, and he believed that it was in our country and the world best interests, to help Europe achieve economic stability.

The Marshall Plan: Restitution and Recovery

Marshall delivered his famous European Recovery Act address at Harvard University's commencement on June 5, 1947. In the following months, Marshall and others drafted a plan that embodied his conviction that economic recovery and stability were vital to the rebuilding of a democratic Europe. A key element in his proposal was that the initiative for reconstruction had to come from the participating countries. America's security and economic prosperity were directly linked to Europe's wellbeing. *www.marshallfoundation.org/TheMarshallPlan.htm*

The Eisenhower Doctrine, 1957 President Dwight D. Eisenhower announced the Eisenhower Doctrine in January 1957, and Congress approved it in March of the same year. 'Under the Eisenhower Doctrine, a country could request American economic assistance and/or aid from U.S. military forces if it was being threatened by armed aggression from another state. Eisenhower singled out the Soviet threat in his doctrine by authorizing the commitment of U.S. forces "to secure and protect the territorial integrity and political independence of such nations, requesting such aid against overt armed aggression from any nation controlled by international communism.' - *http://history.state.gov/milestones/1953-1960/eisenhower-doctrine*.

We always seem to trap of our misleading ego advisor, the echo of the ego. The following table provides a mental and emotional map that links the processes of awareness, reconciliation and forgiveness with elements of the ULC. Laid out is a map of the journey some continents needs to make to find purpose in his or her destiny.

Paradigm Just a Thought

AFRICA	AMERICA- USA	EUROPE	ASIA
Awareness	Awareness	Unity	Awareness
Forgiving	Meaning	Reconciliation	Spiritual science
Rebirth	Enlightenment	Openness	Imagination
Imagination	Reconciliation	Passion	Action
Creation	Imagination	Enlightenment	
Action	Creation		
	Action		
	USA- unity/sharing/awareness		

Imagine: It is remarkable that the United States as well as Europe requires the process of reconciliation before they are able to start the process of forgiveness, or letting go of the past. America first gave meaning to the world when it realized its Marshall Plan in Europe in 1948 till 1951. If the US is able to give meaning back to the world in a new way, it could bring further enlightenment to the world. After shifting perceptions about wellbeing, it could use its imagination and ability to bring new ideas to fruition. To do this, however, the country first needs to transform itself from policeman or to a reconciler that forgive. This country has the experiences [Marshall plan].

The countries and people of Europe need to encounter each other, especially considering their history of disconnection, war and lack of unity. There has been little respect or trust between the cultures and countries of Europe for centuries. Europeans, therefore, need to reconcile with one another to re-activate their soul energy and connect to the passion of the 'we'. Europe should dismantle their bureaucratic governmental structures.

The European Union marks the beginning of a commitment to building unity. However, particularly the European approach keeps it stuck in its tendency to build institutions with too much bureaucracy and too little real human encountering and enlightenment. This is compounded by the egos in the political leadership of various European countries and the arrogance of the new political elite. Trust is often an issue. It is vital for both the US and Europe to go through a process of reconciliation and letting go. Both nations need to let go of the command-and-control approach to leadership and must learn to transcend their egos and cultural arrogance [also true for Russia as part of Asia and Europe]. The Mandela and Gandhi legacy can be helpful here in achieving peaceful transformations.

It is hoped my readers will have seen by now how much the world would benefit from embracing leadership and the awareness of letting go of the past, reconciliation and forgiveness is the way forward to create/innovate new forms of sustainability.

Imagination and the ability to bring new ideas to fruition

Asia should reactivate its ancient wisdom of science. Many Eastern philosophies, such as Taoism, Buddhism and Confucianism, are known for their holistic views and for combining the scientific and the spiritual.

The Not Expected: The Communist Party's third plenum is history - figuratively in that the crucial conclave has concluded and we have the results, and literally in that the transformative vision is truly historic.

In his explanatory address to the party's Central Committee, President Xi Jinping said: "We must waste no time in deepening reform in important areas with even greater political courage and wisdom, firmly do away with all ideological concepts." He stressed that "the development of practice is boundless, liberated thoughts are boundless, reform and opening up are boundless as well; there is no way out in pausing and withdrawing, reforming and opening up only has a progressive tense, not … a perfect tense." These are the strongest words of reform in a generation, a public commitment that sets a high bar to assess policies. *Source: South China Morning Post.*

The Spirit of Time Is Ready for Change!

The new paradigm:

Vision for peace, prosperity and happiness

- Non violence cooperation, the biggest form of war is dialogue
- Less bureaucracy
- Development of a natural economy based on trust and peace
- Understanding of how we really are.

Trinity of three president leaders = The three leaders act as one

How would our world look like if we liberate ourselves from the Babel leadership model the hunter worrier and move to the new form? The thoughts are already at hand from Gandhi, Marshall, Mandela and many others known and unknown.

We can take our individual responsibility and start small in our families, neighborhoods and at work developing new forms of leadership, empowering people getting engage in a natural balanced economy.

13 An encounter with the ULC profiling methodology "Who am I."

This chapter is taking the book to a new level of awareness and an invitation to see. Our focus now returns to the individual, the personal side of the quest for "I am that I am".

We as humans, have an invisible drive to find our full potential. We know instinctively there is something more inside us. We are not always able to find what it is that drives or demotivate us. The activation of our full, unique finger print: The alignment of our inner knowing (subconscious mind), knowing (conscious mind) and our soul, is crucial for our wholeness.

This chapter guides you on completing a personal profile. The Tables used are all contained in the Annexure. Completing a profile assists in aligning your thinking (ego) with your heart energy (inner knowing and soul energy) and also assists in identifying the individual and team emotional restraints and blockages from false belief systems. It opens the inner knowing of our subconscious mind, the unknown self, hidden deep inside us.

This ULC profiling methodology as also available as an App and also for the Android tablet as: "EgosEcho".

A simpler means of profiling oneself, the App contains all Image tables from the ULC etchings in color, Text and illustrations and guides the user, step by step, in how to select and the meaning of the outcome.

The Relationship between the Conscious and Subconscious Mind

William James, the father of American psychology, said that the power to move the world is in your subconscious mind. If we are able to understand and align the interaction between our conscious and subconscious mind, the power released is unimaginable, it's like an erupting volcano of positive energy; creative energy, logic and feelings of joy and harmony.

Joseph Murphy in his booklet: The Power of your Subconscious Mind

It is fascinating and intensely interesting to observe how you can speak authoritatively and with conviction to the irrational movement of your deeper self, bringing silence, harmony, and peace to your mind. The subconscious is subject to the conscious mind. You will perceive the main differences by the following illustrations:

> The conscious mind is like the navigator or captain at the bridge of a ship. He directs the ship and signals orders to men in the engine room, who in turn control all the boilers, instruments, gauges, etc. The men in the engine room do not know where they are going; they follow orders. They would go on the rocks if the man on the bridge issued faulty or wrong instructions based on his findings with the compass, sextant or other instruments. The men in the engine room obey him because he is in charge and issues orders, which are automatically obeyed. Members of the crew do not talk back to the captain; they simply carry out orders. The captain is the master of his ship, and his decrees are carried out.

> Likewise, your conscious mind is the captain and the master of your ship, which represents your body, environment, and all your affairs. Your subconscious mind takes the orders you give it based upon what your conscious mind believes and accepts as true. When you repeatedly say to people, "I can't afford it," then your subconscious mind takes you at your word and sees to it that you will not be in a position to purchase what you want. As long as you persist in saying, "I can't afford that car, that trip to Europe, that home, that fur coat or ermine wrap," you can rest assured that your subconscious mind will follow your orders, and you will go through life experiencing the lack of all the settings.

> Another simple illustration is this: When you say, "I do not like mushrooms," and the occasion subsequently comes that you are served mushrooms in sauces or salads, you will get indigestion because your subconscious mind says to you, "The boss (your conscious mind) does not like mushrooms." This is an amusing example of the outstanding differences and modes of operation of your conscious and subconscious minds.

Source Ailish McGrath (MICHP, ADH)
free down load. www.ichoosetoheal.com
Dr. Joseph Murphy was an Irish born, naturalized American author.

Awaken the Universe Within rather than dream

The Dream comes from the thinking Mind. The Dream is the Mind's reflection of what it wants to manifest in the world, the dreamed action/illusion of the echo of the ego. The dream is also culture related: You must perform, you must become a manager and you want to inspire people and so on. It's your wish of what you would like to see happening in reality, but what is not really you. It is a physical energy that often misleads you, bringing your energy levels down, making you tired sometimes depressed. It is a low frequency. It also represents the potential material/matter limitations of masculine thinking.

In principle be aware that you will never realize the dream in life. This is bold remark. It is the one of peoples miss interpretation of a false believe: 'YOU MUST HAVE A DREAM'. In the many interviews with individuals, explaining the difference between a dream and the inner desire, they suddenly became aware it is true.

You have an inner desire hidden inside you, part of how you really are. This reflects our real purpose, our inner desire. The dream should be replaced by having access to our: 'INNER-DESIRE'

Profiling

I am continually amazed at the response of individuals, as well as management teams, to what the ULC is able to generate from the selections made by the individuals or a collective. "But how did you know?" comes the question. The truth is that a thought is the power of imagination. The ULC has been used for eighteen years in practice in company and society environments, as well with individuals. Because of the individual's interaction with the images during the selection process, the individuals are the ones telling me the story. I merely interpret the etchings shown and put words to them.

The twenty-seven images represent infinite spiral energy; an invitation to see, feel and explore. In the center column are the nine etches, the Source. On the left, Mind Logic, and right, Heart Feeling, are the eighteen etchings.

The original nine etch plates, the Source images, are mirroring the soul's energy in matter in your physical body. The selection of one specific etching reflects the active part, the prevailing energy. The conditioned or suppressed potential is our hidden growth potential personal and/or collective.

The Trinity of the ULC and the twenty-seven images

A few examples:

- Prevent the development, action, or expression of a feeling, impulse, idea, etc.; a restraint: You must listen to the pastor, teacher and so on.
- The thinking and the knowing: Prevent or prohibit someone from doing something due to their dogma's or stigmatization by rhetoric speech.
- Makes someone unable to act in a relaxed and natural way: *his mother's strictures would always inhibit him.*

The Nine Tables

Compiled for the 9 Source Etches and 18 Etchings, there are Nine Tables used to build your full profile:

Table I: Soul (Spiral Energy of the Spirit)

The soul in matter is infinite energy from source, and is not bound by matter. It activates the thinking mind and the feeling heart. This is the individual's unique gift or contribution to the world. This energy also represents our inner Rainmaker.

Table I-a: Soul conditioner

Conditioners are our false believes, dogma's, wrong perceptions, social pressure what is right and what is wrong suppressing, conditioning and blocking us from: Who we really are.

Our personal growth potential is the strength to break through these blockages/conditioners that often give us a feeling of unease. If you open your heart, go with the flow of life, cross the bridge of conditioning, you conquer the resistance that may have been holding you back from who you really are. The image is the etching before the selected soul etches.

Table II: Dream (Mind Energy)

Our dream represents our ego advisor, representing the "I" consciousness. It is that part of us that is the driver of the survival energy. The dream is very often focused on manifesting something in the material world, a concrete or finite goal. Our dream is not in synchronicity with our inner desire, and so it leads us away from the balance we so need inside ourselves. This is the mind "I" ego energy as it sits in matter (brain). It is the inner echo of your ego.

Table III: Inner Knowing (Divine Knowing in matter, our subconscious mind)

Inner knowing is a person's unique fingerprint._This is that intuitive part of us representing our consciousness compass. Our inner knowing is imagination and not always obvious or tangible. This is the soul energy, from source. Its receiver sits in matter in our heart to transform thoughts and infinite wisdom to a form that can be understood by the thinking mind, an alignment of heart (soul) with I (mind). It is the inspiratory of thought and imagination, communicating with our I, our ego. It is your inner Rainmaker in the soul.

The inner knowing bridge is the route to follow to unlock our full potential. Due to conditioning this conscious energy is often hidden very deep inside.

Call it the 'Awakener'.

Table IV: Inner Desire

Inner desire is the energy to support your inner knowing, your essence and purpose in life. It is the intuitive soul, the awareness radar. This energy also represents our inner messenger to support our purpose in this life.

When finding our purpose, when it opens in the self, it is like a tree's buds opening in springtime, showing the trees full potential with all the leaves its fruit, its majestic wonder of life.

It is the start of completion of the aligning of infinite energy of matter in the physical body. The journey can start.

Table V: Talents / Skills

The talents are specific energies that an individual contributes to the collective. From these selections, the individuals will see what they bring to the group setting; this is framed in terms of the Rainmaker, Hunter, and Messenger energies. The talents are the more tangible elements of the individuals' impact on their surroundings.

Table VI: Pitfalls talents/skills

The pitfalls are the obstructions and or conditioners limiting the full energy flow of both our mental, emotional intelligence and the communication with our inner knowing. If individuals are aware of these pitfalls, then they are able to look out for the warning signs bringing unbalanced feelings of unease. Through actively working on those things, being aware that is limiting them. The ULC navigator is a tool for greater self-awareness, assessing the possibilities to better align an individual's talents and abilities. The pitfalls are selected from the eighteen etchings.

Table VII: Mental and Emotional Skills

The mental and emotional skills are those individual abilities that, again, have an impact in the collective setting. They are thinking and feeling abilities, both tangible and intangible, that individuals bring to bear in the group.

Table VIII: Pitfalls Mental & Emotional skills

The pitfalls are the obstructions that can, and do, limit the full energy flow of both the talents and mental and emotional skills. If individuals are aware of these, then they are able to look out for the warning signs or to actively work on those things they know are limiting them. It is a tool for greater self-awareness, assessing the possibilities to better align an individual's talents and abilities. The pitfalls are selected from the eighteen etchings.

Note: Bruce H. Lipton describes in his book, 'The honey moon effect' page nineteen matter as follows: The illustration of the "quantum atom" on the right looks like a mistake- it's blank. That's because quantum physicists have learned that there is no physical substance inside atoms; the subunits that comprise atoms are made out extremely powerful invisible energy vortices, the equivalent of " Nanotornados", not tangible matter. Matter as it turns out, is a strange form of energy: it is not physical.

The Process

The process is metaphysical. It is the sensitivity of the soul's spiral energy (heart) that is communicating with the inner knowing of the individual. These energies will connect and activate the Universe Within.

Each table contains Source etches, with associated Mind and Heart Etchings. What people select comes from inside of them, nowhere else.

Intuitively, without even thinking, using your gut feeling, your intuition, you select one of the nine etches and one of the corresponding etchings. Each of the Etches and Etchings has an interpretation. For Example:

Table VII – The Dream (The Thinking Mind –) select one etch (source)		
1	Not Expected	An individual that wishes to become visionary.
2	Encounter	An individual that wishes to find the energies that binds and inspires people.
3	Transformation	An individual that wishes to formulate realistic and transformative strategies.
4	Movement	An individual that wishes to use his or her practical skills to motivate the collective, to execute the vision and create meaning that resonates in the hearts of the collective.
5	Enlightenment	An individual that wishes that he or she could see things from a helicopter view to ensure that the chosen path will allow for the vision to be realized. Act as a voice that voices the truth.
6	Liberation	An individual that wishes to become the pillar of society. Dreams he/she has the skills to listen to the collective and liberate the people emotionally/mentally from the past.
7	Community	An individual that wishes to unite people to ensure: the people carry the vision.
8	Embracement	An individual that wishes to create Mind in action and Heart in feeling. That there is balance and no domination of the ego, but the unconditional love of the heart embracing the echo of the ego and the ego the heart.
9	Full ending	An individual who wishes he/she is in balance with his body and mind. Mentally / physically and emotionally/spiritually in balance.

Selection Document Profile

The selections from the App or Android tablet are recorded on a profile document.

SOUL: Number etch:			
SOUL CONDITIONER Number before soul etching	Conditioner	Soul etching	

DREAM: Number etch -

INNER KNOWING number etch:			
Inner knowing potential numbers	x	Etch inner knowing	
Inner knowing conditioner bridge	x		

Note: Mark your selection of the right or left etching of the **inner knowing conditioner bridge**.

The selection reflects which side your Inner -knowing is most active. A selection on the left means you will need to cross the bridge from left to right, opening the strength on the right to achieve your full potential. Similarly, for a selection on the left, you will need to develop or access the right column your inner knowing potential for growth. X = selecting the etching in the left column from the selected etch.

INNER DESIRE: Number etch -

PRACTICAL SKILLS – Mark the two selected rows with first and second choice. and The number of the selected etching per row.					
Rainmaker	Hunter	Messenger	Messenger	Hunter	Rainmaker
1	2	3	10	11	12
4	5	6	13	14	15
7	8	9	16	17	18
Pitfall practical select one of the eighteen etchings:					

MENTAL/EMOITIONAL SKILLS - Select two rows mark per Row your selected etching.

A - Hunter	1	2	3
B - Rainmaker	4	5	6
C - Hunter	7	8	9
D – Messenger	10	11	12
E – Messenger	13	14	15
F - Rainmaker	16	17	18
Pitfall mental select one of the eighteen etchings:			

Example Result

Given the number of selections that can be made, this example is summarized. Similarly not all tables are referred to have been presented below (all are in the Annexure).

Miss Y: Profile: Integration Soul and Skills

Selection 1 - Dream: etch 4 Movement

An individual that wishes to use his or her practical skills to motivate the collective, to execute the vision and create meaning that resonates in the hearts of the collective.

Note: Most of the time the dream is using physical energy and makes us tired without a result. This is our echo of the ego advisor in the conscious mind. It is the pressure from the outside world, the thinking and the knowing, how we should behave. In other words, a false belief. The advice should always be: Skip your dream, this gives space in the conscious mind. Namely, the same film without any result, making you tired, is gone. Your real purpose, your unique fingerprint is your inner desire and the inner knowing potential to grow. It is typically hidden due to conditioning deep inside you, your ocean of infinite energy and wisdom: The Universe Within.

Selection 2 - Subconscious mind: The Inner Knowing; etches- 9 Full ending.

18) Full ending—*Kingdom*	9) *Full ending—Kingdom*	9) Full ending—*Kingdom*
This is a stable mind able to pacify the individual as well as the collective. **Miss Y mainly uses her left subconscious wisdom 18and 9**	*The soul's spiral energies in matter find balance in the self. The foundation of a new form of being on a different (higher) level of consciousness.*	The mind is in balance between physical matter and spirit. It brings the feeling processes to completion.
L		X *Potential for growth!!!* R

The above table shows her potential for growth if she brings balance between matter and spirit.

Selection 3 – Inner knowing's conditioner's bridge; she selected etching 18 Full ending left.

This is the indication for what is the conditioned or suppressed part of her inner knowing, namely inner knowing 9 Right above (subconscious mind).

Subconscious: the Inner knowing conditioner's bridge

18) *Full ending—Kingdom*	9) Full ending—*Kingdom*	9) Full ending—*Kingdom*
This is a stable mind able to pacify the individual as well as the collective. **Miss Y: Conditioning energy Search for balance to cross the bridge from L to R Consequence: not fully using her inner knowing 9).**	The soul's spiral energies in matter find balance in the self. The foundation a new form of being on a different (higher) level of consciousness.	The mind is in balance between physical matter and spirit. It brings the feeling processes to completion. *If she arrives in R she develops her full potential of her inner knowing.*
L		R

Selection 4 - Inner desire; etch 5 Enlightenment - Judgment

The soul is aware that there are different levels of consciousness and that there is much more to life than just the world of material. There is also an invisible spiral energy that activates wisdom and the objective judgment of the purpose of being.

Selection 5 - Talents: Rainmaker 18 and second choice messenger 10 (vertical rows)

18 - Always moves through the full cycle, reminding people of the vision and the collective's elevated self

10 - Creates liberation from and a letting go of the past.

Selection 6 – Pitfalls etching 2: Cannot pass through barriers by catalyzing the commitment of the people.

Selection 7 - Mental /Emotional skills (horizontal rows)

10 - Harmony from the heart
9 - Boundary drawing

Selection 8 – Pitfall; etching A1: Shows no emotion

Miss Y's profile is an intriguing one:

She has strong Endurance, not giving up. She can help people to get in balance with the past. She has harmony from the heart, but at a certain moment she draws her boundaries. The reason is that her inner knowing and the inner knowing bridge, are conflicting energies inside her, hampering her from becoming a balanced person. She is struggling with the masculine energy in her subconscious mind. In a world driven by the material she wants to have the image "I am tough" and over reacts on drawing boundaries. She wishes to inspire.

When working on finding our inner knowing conditioner's bridge, crossing it gives us our personal road map for growth.

This spiral energy of our subconscious mind, the inner desire, also represents our inner 'rainmaker-messenger' supporting our inner knowing in the subconscious mind to manifest the invisible on the screen of the conscious mind as imagination, ready for transformation, to give it form in the physical world. (So inside, so outside) It is possible that we are afraid to cross this bridge to our uniqueness.

To go in depth with this analysis is outside the scope of this book, but to create balance she must learn when to let go of drawing boundaries, let go of the dream. This will create the space to come into balance, the energy of the harmony of her heart. In the environment she is working, highly performance/money driven, she might be a gift for the Collective to create a "rainbow nation" working climate.

The value of having such a profile is that it becomes a point of reference. When an individual is able to voice, to put words to an understanding of the self, then they have a kind of road map from which to look at themselves and their place in the world. When we have words or concepts we can use them to make sense of our strengths and talents; we have beacons by which we can navigate our way in the world. The individual and collective interact, interface, shape, and are shaped by one another. This is where the deeper value of doing individual selections manifests as a benefit to a fuller person and understanding of the collective picture.

The above is meant as an appetizer. I invite you to experience the ULC Navigator in practice with the "EgosEcho" Apple's APP and the Google Android tablet, allowing you to dig deeper into all tables, images and interpretations to find who we are and what is your destination'

Gregg Braden in his book the Turning Point

> I see a better place for us all.
>
> *I see a world where we've raised the standard of living for everyone, rather than lowering it for many in order to support only a few.*
>
> And I see the shift in thinking that makes each of these things possible. To get to that shift, however, we must begin by recognizing the realities that we face and the promise that they hold.

Awaken the Universe Within
With respect and love for life, Willem.

Annexure

The Nine Tables

Table I: Active Soul's spiral energy: select one of the etches from the source

First select one of the 9 Source etches, then one of the associated etchings from the left or right.

Source: Next to etch **1** are the etchings 17+3 This row of three represents the soul's full potential. Source: Next to etch **2** are the etchings 6+2 and so on.		Soul: Etching 1 till 18 Selection of the active part of our soul's energy select one etching A or B. A: feminine energy/ subconscious mind more at play/right brain *B: masculine energy, conscious mind more at play/left brain*
1	Not Expected	A-17) The Soul has the ability to see into the future and to receive a new thought seeming coming out of nowhere. B- 3) The soul's spiral has the ability to free the mind from the past, creating space for an awakening.
2	Encounter	6) The soul is able to sense and gain insight into the emotional blockages within a collective or individual human being. 2) The mind has an intuitive radar talent for finding the energies that binds the individual persons as well individuals in a collective.
3	Transformation	4) The Soul can transmute the thought into a meaningful concepts/ideas that can easily be understood by the individual as well a collective or society. 15) The mind has the ability to formulate the thought into a realistic plan that is identity and awareness orientated.
4	Movement	11) The Soul can convert thoughts into meaning that resonates in the hearts of the collective, motivating and inspiring the individuals. 5) The mind is able to take visionary thoughts/vision and motive people through down to earth strategies to manifest action.
5	Enlightenment	10) The soul senses if the chosen path is in balance with the wellbeing of the Collective. 8) The mind has the ability to take a helicopter view and reflect on it.
6	Liberation	7) The soul uses its remarkable listening energies and intuitive ability to create a relationship of trust within the Collective, reducing fear through the soul's spiral energy of unconditional love, shining of the light within. 13) The mind has the skills to liberate itself and the Collective from the past.
7	Community	1) The Soul has the energy to create unity (Trinity) and manifesting the alignment of heart and mind energies. 16) The soul using the logic of the mind to unify people making them aware of and understanding the reality (truth).
8	Embracement	12) The soul embraces the Ego (Mind), and support of the ego in action with the positive energy flow of unconditional love. (Power of harmony) 14) The enlightened ego embraces the heart in humility. *Risk the mind's rationality dominates, activating ' the echo of the ego's' energy of arrogance and duality.*
9	Full ending	9) The Soul's energy is in spiritual and emotional balance (matter). 18) The mind's rational/logic ego energy is a balanced energy in the material world. (Physical matter)

Table Ia: Soul's Conditioner is the etching before the selected soul etching

Example:

If you selected **etch 4- Movement** as your **full soul** potential. You than take **etching 5-Movement** as your **active soul energy** (*not: 11 Movement*) than **etching 4** the transformation is your **conditioner**.

Soul etch	Conditioners: etchings 1 to 18 reflecting souls conditioned energy
1-Not Expected	17) The Soul has difficulties to see into the future and to create new thoughts to give space in the mind for hoop. 3) The mind is not able to free itself from the past, creating the space for an awakening. The mind is more or less bound to live in the prison of the past.
2-Encounter	6) The soul has difficulties in sensing or gaining insight into the emotional blockages within the other person or collective. 2) The mind has difficulties to find the energy that bind the Collective or the other person. Soloist mind.
3-Transformation	4) The Soul has difficulties to transmute a thought into meaningful concepts that can be easily understood by other people. 15) The mind has not the ability to transmute the thought into a plan that is identity or awareness related.
4-Movement	11) The Soul has difficulties creating meaning that resonates in people's hearts and /or inspires people's soul. 5) The mind is not able to take visionary ideas and transmute them into realistic action.
5-Enlightenment	10) The soul has problems with reflection if the chosen path is in balance with the wellbeing of the collective. 8) The Soul has difficulties to take a helicopter view. Her conditioners freeze the soul's energy to awaken.
6 Liberation	7) A soul is struggling with listening, believe in his/her ability to create a relationship of trust with the other person and/ or collective. 13) The mind has difficulties to liberate itself and/or the collective from the past.
7 Community	1) The soul's energy is not able to unify through unconditional love –alignment of Heart and Mind energies. Not able to access the power of subconscious inner knowing 16) The mind is not able to create unity between opponents.
8-Embracement	12) The soul (heart) has difficulties to embrace the ego (mind), as a welcome guest in support of action. (Feeling not at ease) 14) The mind's ego is not able to pacify.
9-Full ending	9) The Soul has difficulties with finding the spiritual and/or emotional balance. 18) The mind is not in balance with the materialistic world. Difficult to letting go the echo of ego. (Focused on rationality/economical results/having financial value).

Table II: Mind's Dream - Select one etch
Example Etch selection 1- Not expected:
The dream - An individual that wishes to become visionary

Table 2 – The Dream (The Thinking Mind –) select one etch (source)		
1	Not Expected	An individual that wishes to become visionary and creative.
2	Encounter	An individual that wishes to find the energies that binds and inspires people.
3	Transformation	An individual that wishes to formulate realistic and transformative strategies.
4	Movement	An individual that wishes to use his or her practical skills to motivate the collective to execute the vision and create meaning that resonates in the hearts of the collective.
5	Enlightenment	An individual that wishes to that he or she could see things from a helicopter view to ensure that the chosen path will allow for the vision to be realized. Act as a voice that voices the truth.
6	Liberation	An individual that wishes to become the pillar of society. Dreams he/she has the skills to listen to the collective and liberate the people emotionally/mentally from the past.
7	Community	An individual that wishes to unite people to ensure: That the people carry the vision.
8	Embracement	An individual that wishes to create mind in action and Heart in feeling. That there is balance and no domination of the ego. The heart embracing the echo of the ego and the ego embracing the heart.
9	Full ending	An individual who wishes he/she is in balance with his body and mind. Physical matter and souls spirit and emotions are in balance.

Table III: Inner Knowing and inner knowing's conditioner bridge selections

Inner Knowing

8) Enlightenment—*Judgment*	1) Not expected—*Wisdom*	10) Enlightenment—*Judgment*
This mind has the ability to take a helicopter view and is able to create awareness of the reality. Left	This soul's inner knowing can free the conscious mind from conditioning. Visionary energy is unleashed. The soul's taps in the ocean of wisdom. Thoughts can be received and transmuted.	The mind feels if the road ahead is in balance with the well being of the collective. Right

Conditioner – Bridge: select right or left etching

3) Not expected—*Wisdom*	5) *Enlightenment- Judgment*	17) Not Expected—*Wisdom*
The mind has the ability to empty the memory box of the conscious mind Left	*The soul is aware that there are different levels of consciousness and that there is much more to life than just the world of physical matter. There is also an invisible spiral energy that activates wisdom and the objective judgment of the purpose of being.*	This mind has the capability to free itself from the past, creating the space for an awakening. Opening the doors to receive the invisible infinite thought energy creating new forms. Right

Inner Knowing

5) Movement—*Mercy*	2) Encounter—*Understanding*	11) Movement—*Mercy*
This mind is being able to take the visionary ideas and transmute the thought in a realistic action. Down-to-earth solution. L	This soul can create understanding. The soul is in dialogue with its subconscious and conscious mind. Creates form. Identity.	This mind can convert the thought into meaning that resonates in the hearts of the collective. The feeling is good and reduces fear. This mind is able to unlock the leader in each person. R

Conditioner-Bridge: select right or left etching

2) Encounter—*Understanding*	8) *Embracement—Foundation*	6) Encounter—*Understanding*
This mind has a radar talent for finding the energies or understands what bind the collective. L	*The soul's energy embraces the conscious and subconscious mind as necessary and enjoyable partners, not as opponents that must be defeated. The universal power of polarity.*	The mind is able to sense the emotional/mental blockages within the collective or an individual. R

Inner Knowing

14) Embracement- *Foundation* The enlightened mind's ego embraces the heart in humility. When the ego is lacking enlightenment, then this can lead to arrogance or dominance of the 'I'. L	3) Transformation—*Knowledge* This soul inner knowing, through its awareness of the truth, allows for the letting go of the past. Trust can emerge.	12) Embracement -*Foundation* The mind's unconditional love embraces the ego (Love in support of action). Confidence in the 'I' and 'We'. R

Conditioner-Bridge: select right or left etching

15) Transformation- *Knowledge* This mind has the ability to formulate the thought into a logic plan that strengthen the identity and is perceived as realistic. L	6) *Liberation—Beauty* *The souls noble guest of forgiveness knocks on the door of the mind. In order to be able to forgive in the world one must achieve forgiveness in the self. The invisible power letting go the conditioners of the past.*	4) Transformation-*Knowledge* This mind has a giving energy, willing to share knowledge to transmute thoughts, feelings, into meaningful concepts that can easily understood by people. Giving confidence. R

Inner Knowing

13) Liberation—*Beauty* This mind has the skills to liberate itself and the collective or individual from the past. This mind has the unifying energy to empower the 'I' and inviting the ego as a welcome guest. L	4) Movement—*Mercy* The soul recognizes the truth in itself by coming in dialogue with this inner knowing. The soul has the wisdom to create meaning.	7) Liberation—*Beauty* The mind uses its remarkable listening sensors and intuitive ability to create a relationship of trust with the collective or individual, reducing fear through love. R

Conditioner-Bridge: select right or left etching

5) Movement—*Mercy* This mind is being able to take the visionary ideas and transmute the thought in a realistic action. Down-to-earth solution. L	2) *Encounter—Understanding* *This soul can create understanding. The soul is in dialogue with its subconscious and conscious mind. Creates form. Identity.*	11) Movement—*Mercy* This mind can convert the thought into meaning that resonates in the hearts of the collective. The feeling is good and reduces fear. This mind is able to unlock the leader in each person. R

Inner Knowing

3) Not expected—*Wisdom* The mind has the ability to empty the memory box of the conscious mind	5) Enlightenment-*Judgment* The soul is aware that there are different levels of consciousness and that there is much more to life than just the world of physical matter. There is also an invisible spiral energy that activates wisdom and the objective judgment of the purpose of being.	17) Not Expected—*Wisdom* This mind has the capability to free itself from the past, creating the space for an awakening. Opening the doors to receive the invisible infinite thought energy creating new forms.

Conditioner-Bridge: select right or left etching

8) Enlightenment—*Judgment* This mind has the ability to take a helicopter view and is able to create awareness of the reality.	1) *Not expected—Wisdom This soul's inner knowing can free the conscious mind from conditioning. Visionary energy is unleashed. The soul's taps in the ocean of wisdom. Thoughts can be received and transmuted.*	10) Enlightenment—*Judgment* The mind feels if the road ahead is in balance with the well being of the collective.

Inner Knowing

15) Transformation- *Knowledge* This mind has the ability to formulate the thought into a logic plan that strengthen the identity and is perceived as realistic.	6) Liberation—*Beauty* The souls noble guest of forgiveness knocks on the door of the mind. In order to be able to forgive in the world one must achieve forgiveness in the self. The invisible power letting go the conditioners of the past.	4) Transformation-*Knowledge* This mind has a giving energy, willing to share knowledge to transmute thoughts, feelings, into meaningful concepts that can easily understood by people. Giving confidence.

Conditioner-Bridge: select right or left etching

13) Liberation—*Beauty* This mind has the skills to liberate itself and the collective or individual from the past. This mind has the unifying energy to empower the 'I' and inviting the ego as a welcome guest.	4) *Movement—Mercy The soul recognizes the truth in itself by coming in dialogue with this inner knowing. The soul has the wisdom to create meaning.*	7) Liberation—*Beauty* The mind uses its remarkable listening sensors and intuitive ability to create a relationship of trust with the collective or individual, reducing fear through love.

Inner Knowing

16) Community—*Eternity* This mind has the energy to create unity through creating awareness of purpose of the community.	7) Community—*Eternity* The soul through its unconditional love energy, releases in the self, the community a climate/feeling of trust, sharing the truth The soul's spiral energy gives the feeling we are united we are one.	1) Community—*Eternity* A mind being able to unify the collective. Manifesting alignment of heart and mind the feeling of belonging.

Conditioner-Bridge: select right or left etching

16) Community—*Eternity* This mind has the energy to create unity through creating awareness of purpose of the community.	7) *Community—Eternity The soul through its unconditional love energy, releases in the self, the community a climate/feeling of trust, sharing the truth The soul's spiral energy gives the feeling we are united we are one.*	1) Community—*Eternity* A mind being able to unify the collective. Manifesting alignment of heart and mind the feeling of belonging.

Inner Knowing

2) Encounter—*Understanding* This mind has a radar talent for finding the energies or understands what bind the collective.	8) Embracement—*Foundation* The soul's energy embraces the conscious and subconscious mind as necessary and enjoyable partners, not as opponents that must be defeated. The universal power of polarity.	6) Encounter—*Understanding* The mind is able to sense the emotional/mental blockages within the collective or an individual.

Conditioner-Bridge: select right or left etching

14) Embracement- *Foundation* The enlightened mind's ego embraces the heart in humility. When the ego is lacking enlightenment, then this can lead to arrogance or dominance of the 'I'.	3) *Transformation—Knowledge This soul inner knowing, through its awareness of the truth, allows for the letting go of the past. Trust can emerge.*	12) Embracement -*Foundation* The mind's unconditional love embraces the ego (Love in support of action). Confidence in the 'I' and 'We'.

Inner Knowing

18) **Full ending—*Kingdom*** This is a stable mind able to pacify the individual as well as the collective.	9) **Full ending—*Kingdom*** The soul's spiral energies in matter find balance in the self. The foundation a new form of being on a different (higher) level of consciousness.	9) **Full ending—*Kingdom*** The mind is in balance between physical matter and spirit. It brings the feeling processes to completion.

Conditioner-Bridge: select right or left etching

18) **Full ending—*Kingdom*** This is a stable mind able to pacify the individual as well as the collective.	9) *Full ending—Kingdom The soul's spiral energies in matter find balance in the self. The foundation a new form of being on a different (higher) level of consciousness.*	9) **Full ending—*Kingdom*** The mind is in balance between physical matter and spirit. It brings the feeling processes to completion.

Table IV –Your Inner desire?
Select one etches from the source.

1) **Not expected—*Wisdom***
This soul's inner knowing can free the conscious mind from conditioning. Visionary energy is unleashed. The soul's taps in the ocean of wisdom. Thoughts can be received and transmuted

2) **Encounter—*Understanding***
This soul can create understanding. The soul is in dialogue with its subconscious and conscious mind. Creates form and Identity.

3) **Transformation—*Knowledge***
This soul inner knowing, through its awareness of the truth, allows for the letting go of the past. Trust can emerge.

4) **Movement—*Mercy***
The soul recognizes the truth in itself by coming in dialogue with this inner knowing. The soul has the wisdom to create meaning.

5) **Enlightenment- *Judgment***
The soul is aware that there are different levels of consciousness and that there is much more to life than just the world of physical matter. There is also an invisible spiral energy that activates wisdom and the objective judgment of the purpose of being

6) **Liberation—*Beauty***
The souls noble guest of forgiveness knocks on the door of the mind. In order to be able to forgive in the world one must achieve forgiveness in the self. The invisible power letting go the conditioners of the past.

7) **Community—*Eternity***
The soul through its unconditional love energy, releases in the self, the community a climate/feeling of trust, sharing the truth The soul's spiral energy gives the feeling we are united we are one

8) **Embracement—*Foundation***
The soul's energy embraces the conscious and subconscious mind as necessary and enjoyable partners, not as opponents that must be defeated. The universal power of polarity. United in diversity.

9) **Full ending—*Kingdom***
The soul's spiral energies in matter find balance in the self. The foundation a new form of being on a different (higher) level of consciousness.

Table V: The Practical Skills/Talents
Example: Selections row B 11 and row F 15 this are your talents

A Rainmaker energy	B Hunter energy	C Messenger energy
1 Inspires the collective with the basic idea or thought.	2 Passes through barriers by catalyzing the commitment of the people to execute the thought/vision.	3 Acts a steward for reconciliation and forgiveness. The custodian of the truth and living in harmony.
4 Shifts perceptions through his natural giving energy of unconditional love for humanity.	5 Makes clear what kind of commitment is needed and what has to be done to realize the vision.	6 Listens through the collective to understand if the vision is still alive or if there are still blockages from the pain of the past.
7 Creates space for change and unity.	8 Reflects on a strategy to see if it is in line with the objectives of the vision.	9 Creates a climate favorable to encourage harmony with the past.

Continuation Table V D Messenger energy	E Hunter energy	F Rainmaker energy
10 Creates liberation from, and a letting go of, the past.	11 Realizing the vision through tangible results. Has the energy of reloading himself with positive energy after a disappointment.	12 Acts as the soul of society and protects the collective from stigmatization through awareness and living in harmony with the past.
13 Reflects on the past to see if the liberation is a reality.	14 By realizing/bringing the results there is the risk of becoming arrogant: I am the best.	15 Acts as guardian of elevated consciousness: The "we" embracing the "I."
16 Creates unities wherein the vision is embraced by the people. Awareness for caring.	17 Achieves more than is expected through being driven by incredibly high standards to perform as collective. Risk of being dominant, overpowering.	18 Always moves through the full cycle, reminding people of the vision and the collective's elevated self.

Table VI The Pitfalls of the Skills/Talents
Select one of the eighteen etchings **you don't like**
Example: Your selection 13 is your Pitfall

1 Cannot inspire the collective with the basic idea.	2 Cannot pass through barriers by catalyzing the commitment of the people.	3 Cannot act as a steward for reconciliation and forgiveness.
4 Cannot shift perceptions.	5 Cannot make clear what kind of commitment is needed and what has to be done to realize the vision	6 Cannot listen through the collective to understand if the vision is still alive or if there are still blockages from the pain of the past.
7 Cannot create space for change and unity.	8 Cannot reflect on a strategy to see if it is in line with the objective of the vision.	9 Cannot create a climate favorable to encourage harmony with the past.
10 Cannot create liberation from and a letting go of the past.	11 Cannot realize the vision through tangible results.	12 Cannot act as the soul of society and protect the collective from stigmatization through awareness and living in harmony with the past.
13 Cannot reflect on the past to see if the liberation is a reality.	14 Cannot give the collective the opportunity to move to a higher level of consciousness.	15 Cannot act as guardian of a higher consciousness: The we embracing the I.
16 Cannot create unity where the people embrace the vision.	17 Cannot achieve; a higher level of consciousness creating space to life in harmony.	18 Cannot move through the full cycle, reminding people of the vision and the Collective's higher self.

Table VII The Mental/Emotional skills
Select two horizontal rows (vertical columns). Select one image per selected row.
Example, row D, image 11; and row F, image 18.This are your skills

A	1 Emotion	2 Senses	3 Intuition
B	4 Deep thinking	5 Spirituality	6 Great wisdom to avoid arrogance
C	7 Boundary—shifting	8 Liberation	9 Boundary drawing
D	10 Harmony from the heart	11 Responsibility	12 Ethical and moral choices
E	13 Stability	14 Reliability—being the cornerstone of society	15 A disciplined moderator
F	16 Creativity of mind and soul	17 Energy of innocence/flexible	18 Talent for addressing people and/or writing

Table VIII: The Mental/Emotional Pitfalls,
Select one of the 18 etchings you *don't* like
Example: Select 7 that is your pitfall.

A	1 Shows no emotion	2 Weak senses	3 Has no intuition
B	4 Unable to think deeply	5 Not spiritual	6 Not wise and is arrogant
C	7 Unable to shift boundaries	8 Not liberated	9 Unable to set boundaries
D	10 No harmony from the heart	11 Does not take responsibility	12 Does not make ethical and moral choices
E	13 Not stable	14 Unreliable—not a cornerstone of society	15 Not a disciplined moderator
F	16 Not creative in mind or soul	17 Not flexible/suspicious	18 No talent for writing and/or / speech

Disclaimer
This document intended for the App and Android user's eyes only. Miss- interpretation of the images in this book is at users own responsibility. The reason the colors of the App reflects the colors of the authentic art. All images registered as trademark ®

Bibliography

Chapter 1
Professor Bruce Lipton: *The Biology of Belief*
Quote Carl Jung: *Who looks outside, dreams. Who looks inside, awakens.*
Albert Einstein: *The intuitive mind is a sacred gift and the rational mind is a faithful servant*

Chapter 2
Jan Monty: Etchings trinity ULC
'Spiral Dynamics' written by D.E Beck and Ch. C Cowan they write: "In his book '*Cycles*'
Samuel A Schreiner, Jr. invites the reader to discover 'Cycleland'

Chapter 3
W.H.J de Liefde: Lekgotla: *The Art of Leadership through Dialogue.*
Dr. Maki Mandela wrote the following passage in that book:
It is for those who are willing to dig deeper, to look beyond the surface of things.
W.H.J. de Liefde: *ULC- The Leadership Navigator*
Professor van der Merwe: Constructed an ingenious matrix he calls the Universal Life Cycle
    (ULC) to help you understand yourself, your team, and your company
D. L. Jewett, in "What's Wrong With Single Hypotheses"
Quote Lemaseya Khama - Gaborone, Botswana. *The Western mindset places a greater
    emphasis on the "I," the healing of the individual, whereas we Africans believe that if the
    community is healed, we as individuals are healed in the process.*

Chapter 4
Machiavelli's greatest insight for ego driven organizations

Chapter 5
Tolstoy shared his insight on the topic of thought
Quote of Deepak Chopra: Every time you are tempted to react in....
Quote of Martha Graham (dancer and choreographer) *"There is a vitality, a life force* Drunvalo
    Melchizedek writes on the Internet about enlightenment.

Plato: Know thyself

Chapter 6
Byron Katie: Loving What Is
Thich Nhat Hanh refers to this as "the knots of anger,"
Don E. Beck and Christopher C. Cowan: Spiral Dynamics
Nelson Mandela, Inaugural Address, Pretoria 9 May 1994
Obama's first inaugural
Emil Protalinski: Iceland taps Facebook to rewrite its constitution
Laurence van der Post and Jane Taylor: Testament to the Bushman

Chapter 7
Psychologist Jeanne Lu Bruwer *Employees need to feel that there is a platform for their voices....*
Unilever chief Paul Polman talks to Jo Confino: About the company's radical sustainability agenda
Laurence van der Post and Jane Taylor: Testament to the Bushma
Quotes identity phase of: Archbishop Buti Tlhagale , Khali Gibran and Lao Tzu

Chapter 8:
Quote Martin Luther King: *Men often hate each other because*
Louis Liebenberg, in The Art of Tracking: The Origin of Science

Chapter 9
Robert Ohotto in *Fate into Destiny*
Booklet Rio Tinto Mining Palabora, South Africa printed and designed by the Kgotla Company, Amsterdam

Chapter 10
Quote: Lucy Maud Montgomery: *There is so much in the world for all of us...*
Quotes meaning phase of:_Obama, Williamson, Plato

Chapter 11
Quotes collective phase of: Chief Seattle, **Muhammad** Rumi , Roberto Assagioli
Paul Schilpp, 1979, Albert Einstein: Autobiographical Notes.
Quote Mahatma Gandhi: Happiness is when what you think .....
Quote Albert Einstein : *All these primary impulses.....*

Chapter 13
The Marshall Plan: Restitution and Recovery

Chapter 14
Bruce H. Lipton describes in: The honey-moon effect
Dr. Joseph Murphy in: The Power of your Sub-Conscious Mind

Acknowledgments

A word of thanks to the following people:

Phil Connolly, my sounding board and advisor on the logic flow of the content.

Martijn, a firm believer in the ULC/KGOTLA philosophy and ULC profiling methodology.

Martijn de Liefde – the Kgotla company
Amsterdam, The Netherlands

Special thanks to these supporters:

Alf McKnight
Chantal Sturkenboom
Howard Drakes and
Anoek Hoijting
for their structural input
and all who listened to me.

And special thanks to the creators of the artwork:

Jan Montijn, Amsterdam NL (etchings ULC)
Michel van Overbeeke, Haarlem NL (paintings)
Klaus Elle, Hamburg DE (sketches)

About the Author

Willem H. J. de Liefde was born in Coevorden, The Netherlands. His working life started as an officer in the merchant marine. He ended his naval career as an officer in the Royal Dutch Navy. Afterward, he studied economics and held several management and directorships in Europe, the United States, and Africa, working for multinationals as such as Ericsson, Rank Xerox, Rockwool, and Draeger. His expertise is in managing transformation and inspiring people. His best results are achieved through sharing the truth, through intuition, and through using art as a hidden message.

Willem has written several books on leadership and working together:

- *Lekgotla: The Art of Leadership through Dialogue* (Jacana). A ground breaking book, its title, *Lekgotla*, is a Sesotho word for "meeting circle or assembly."
- *ULC—The Leadership Navigator: Governance without Fear* (Jacana).
- "African tribal leadership voor Westerse managers" (Kluwer).
- "Ubuntu" (Signum bei Herbig) language German.

The art of the Universal Life Cycle, used in all his books, is a powerful diagnostic tool. In this book, *Awaken the Universe Within*, it is used to help you understand who you are and your inner drivers, being your soul, your inner knowing, and your talents. This book is also about better understanding the other person. The author's philosophy behind this concept is that if you don't know who you are—your identity—you cannot give meaning to life, and without meaning, you cannot lead people or yourself.

From the writers desk:

This book is about: The power of thought. "Who am I" is the journey of the leader inside you, discovering your full human potential, unlocking the power with in you. The Universal Life Cycle guides you and your organization in the process of unlocking your full human potential. The thought energy inside Collectives is the differentiator of positive energy within organizations to create admiration, innovation, passion and a vision carried by the people.

It also about: Empowering and awakening a person through intriguing point of views as to how a person can become a master of the talents he has and who he really is. Accessing the ocean of wisdom and creativity, our subconscious minds, our inner knowing.

For more information, please contact the following:
Willem de Liefde
Warmond , The Netherlands

www.EgosEcho.com

willem@egosecho.com
Profiling tool:
APP and Android tablet- title: "*EgosEcho*"

Author